The HUMAN ENVIRONMENT

CALVIN CLARKE

STANDARD GRADE GEOGRAPHY

Hodder & Stoughton
A MEMBER OF THE HODDER HEADLINE GROUP

ACKNOWLEDGEMENTS

The publishers would like to thank the following individuals, institutions and companies for permission to reproduce photographs in this book. Every effort has been made to trace ownership of copyright. The publishers would be happy to make arrangements with any copyright holder whom it has not been possible to contact:

J. Allan Cash Ltd (29 bottom); Calvin Clarke (37 all photos, 79, 80, 88); Carlisle City Council (29 top); Corbis (16, 20 bottom left, 43, 85, 104, 105); Honda (77); Hulton Getty (20 top right, 46); Lancashire County Library (20 middle right); National Power (67); Newcastle Libraries and Information Services (69); Scotland in Focus Picture Library/A.G. Firth (35); Scottish Borders Tourist Board (27); Sealand Aerial Photography Ltd (53); Tom Walsh (20 bottom right)

British Library Cataloguing in Publication Data
A catalogue record for this title is available from The British Library

ISBN 0 340 69089 5

First published 1998
Impression number 10 9 8 7 6 5 4 3
Year 2002 2001 2000

Cover photo from Robert Harding Picture Library/Nigel Francis
Illustrations by Chartwell Illustrators, 406A Brighton Road, South Croydon, Surrey CR2 6AN.

Typeset by Fakenham Photosetting Limited, Fakenham, Norfolk NR21 8NL.
Printed in Great Britain for Hodder & Stoughton Educational, a division of Hodder Headline Plc, 338 Euston Road, London NW1 3BH by Redwood Books Ltd, Trowbridge, Wiltshire.

CONTENTS

INTRODUCTION

STRUCTURE

This book is designed for pupils of all abilities to learn key ideas 7–11 of the Scottish Standard Grade syllabus and to develop the gathering and processing techniques prescribed in the syllabus. The book is divided into fifteen units and each unit is divided into several sections:

1 all pupils read the **Core text**
2 all pupils answer the **Core questions**.
Pupils then choose to
3 answer the **Foundation questions**
or
4 answer the **General questions**
or
5 read the **Extension text** and answer the **Extension questions** and the **Credit questions**.

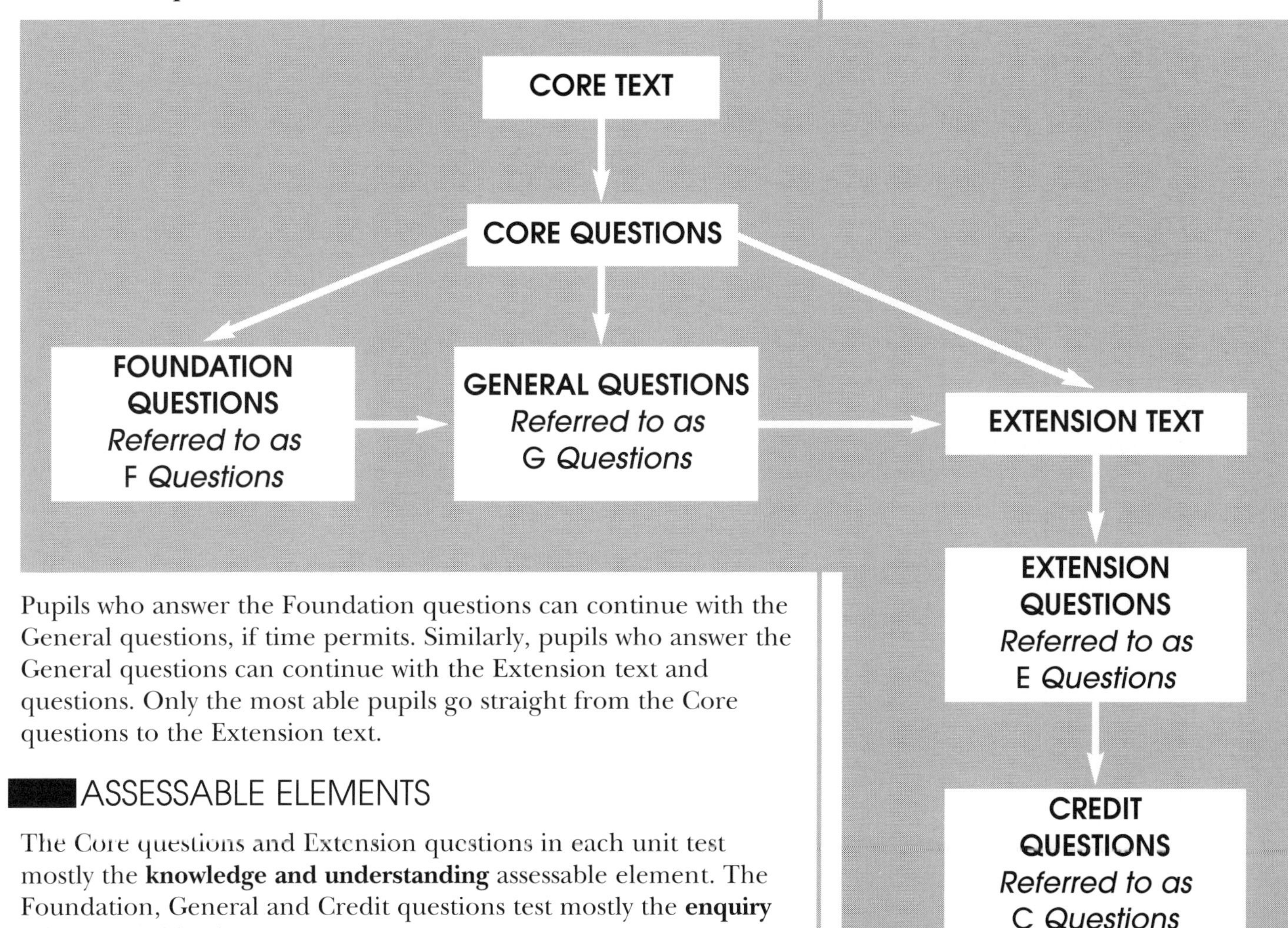

Pupils who answer the Foundation questions can continue with the General questions, if time permits. Similarly, pupils who answer the General questions can continue with the Extension text and questions. Only the most able pupils go straight from the Core questions to the Extension text.

ASSESSABLE ELEMENTS

The Core questions and Extension questions in each unit test mostly the **knowledge and understanding** assessable element. The Foundation, General and Credit questions test mostly the **enquiry skills** assessable element.

Unit	Key Ideas	Knowledge and Understanding (F/G levels)			Knowledge and Understanding (G/C levels)			Enquiry Skills (F level)					Enquiry Skills (G level)					Enquiry Skills (C level)				
		a	b	c	a	b	c	a	b	c	d	e	a	b	c	d	e	a	b	c	d	e
1	7/8			✔			✔				✔	✔				✔	✔				✔	✔
2	7	✔	✔		✔	✔	✔	✔		✔			✔	✔	✔			✔	✔			
3	7	✔	✔		✔	✔		✔	✔	✔			✔	✔				✔		✔		
4	8	✔	✔			✔		✔		✔			✔	✔				✔		✔		
5	8	✔	✔		✔	✔		✔		✔			✔	✔	✔			✔	✔	✔		
6	10/11			✔			✔				✔	✔				✔	✔				✔	✔
7	10	✔	✔		✔	✔		✔					✔	✔				✔		✔		
8	10	✔	✔			✔		✔		✔			✔		✔			✔		✔		
9	10	✔	✔		✔	✔		✔		✔			✔	✔				✔	✔	✔		
10	11	✔	✔		✔		✔	✔		✔			✔	✔				✔		✔		
11	9			✔			✔				✔	✔				✔	✔				✔	✔
12	4/9	✔	✔			✔		✔		✔			✔	✔	✔			✔		✔		
13	4/9	✔	✔		✔			✔	✔	✔			✔	✔	✔			✔	✔	✔		
14	5/11	✔	✔		✔			✔					✔	✔				✔	✔	✔		
15		✔			✔			✔	✔	✔			✔	✔	✔			✔	✔	✔		

UNIT 1

Skills in Urban Studies

Core text

1A INTRODUCTION TO URBAN STUDIES

Geography involves the study of **landscapes**. Landscapes can be **physical landscapes** (such as mountains and rivers) or **human landscapes** (landscapes made by people). **Urban studies** are studies of towns and cities. Towns and cities are one of the more striking ways in which people have changed and shaped the landscape. For the Standard Grade examination, you need to know and understand:

1 where settlements first began;
2 the reasons why settlements have grown;
3 the different functions of settlements;
4 the spheres of influence of settlements and services;
5 the main land uses in towns and their locations;
6 the changes in land use at the edge of towns;
7 the causes of and solutions to traffic congestion;
8 the causes of and solutions to urban decay.

You also need to develop the following enquiry skills:

1 how and where to gather information on towns, by undertaking surveys and questionnaires;
2 how to process the information, by drawing bar graphs and scattergraphs;
3 how to analyse the information.

The rest of this unit deals with ways of gathering and processing information about towns.

1B GATHERING INFORMATION

There are many different ways of finding out information about towns. They are called **gathering techniques**. For example, to investigate the topics studied for Standard Grade, some of the techniques that can be used are:

Figure 1.1

Topic studied	Gathering technique
Settlement site	**Fieldsketching** – drawing a sketch of the site **Extracting information from maps** on height, slope and aspect
Settlement growth and function	**Observing and recording** buildings – their uses and ages
Spheres of influence	**Compiling and using a questionnaire** with local shoppers **Interviewing** shopkeepers
Land uses in towns	**Observing and recording** land uses **Extracting information from maps**
Urban decay	**Observing and recording** environmental quality **Interviewing** local people
Traffic	**Observing and recording** traffic flows

1C OBSERVING AND RECORDING TRAFFIC FLOW

You can observe and record traffic flow by counting the number of vehicles passing a given point for a set amount of time (called a **traffic survey**) like the one in Figure 1.2 below. Before you begin a traffic survey, you need to ask yourself some questions.

TRAFFIC SURVEY RECORD SHEET					
Date: 6 May 1998			Location: Dumbarton Road, outside Littlewoods		
Start Time: 2.00 pm			Finish Time: 2.30 pm		
cars	buses	lorries	vans	motorbikes	bikes
⁄⁄⁄⁄ ⁄⁄⁄⁄ ⁄⁄⁄⁄ ⁄⁄⁄⁄ ⁄⁄⁄⁄ ⁄⁄⁄⁄ ⁄⁄⁄⁄ ⁄⁄⁄⁄ ⁄⁄⁄⁄ ⁄⁄⁄⁄ ⁄⁄⁄⁄ ⁄⁄⁄⁄ ⁄⁄⁄⁄ ⁄⁄⁄⁄ ⁄⁄⁄⁄ ⁄⁄⁄⁄ ⁄⁄⁄⁄ ⁄⁄⁄⁄ III	⁄⁄⁄⁄ ⁄⁄⁄⁄ ⁄⁄⁄⁄ I	⁄⁄⁄⁄	⁄⁄⁄⁄ ⁄⁄⁄⁄ II	IIII	⁄⁄⁄⁄ ⁄⁄⁄⁄

Figure 1.2

- Where should I stand to count the traffic?
  The amount of traffic may vary at different places along the street. You might want to choose the busiest area, or count the traffic at several places.
- Which day of the week shall I do the survey?
  Some days are busier than others. You might want to choose the busiest day or count the traffic on different days.
- What time of day should I choose?
  Some times of day are much busier than others.
- Should I count traffic in both directions or just one?
  One direction may be much busier than the other, especially at rush hour.

- Should I count all the vehicles?
  There will be cars, buses, lorries, vans, motorbikes and bicycles. You might want to count each type of vehicle separately.
- For how long should I count the traffic?
  If you count for just a few minutes, it may produce an unreliable or 'fluke' result. You should count at each site for at least 10 minutes.

1D COMPILING AND USING A QUESTIONNAIRE

SHOPPING HABITS QUESTIONNAIRE

Date: 5 February 1998 Location: Near Boots, Milngavie

Time: 11.00 am

Excuse me, I'm doing some work for my Geography course at school. Would you mind answering a few questions?

1 Do you normally shop at this centre?
2 In which street do you live?
3 What means of transport did you use to get here?
4 How often do you shop here?
5 Which shops will you be using?
6 Why do you use this shopping centre?

Question	Person 1	Person 2	Person 3	Person 4	Person 5	Person 6	Person 7
1	yes	yes	yes				
2	Hunter Road	Lynn Drive	Mugdock Road				
3	car	car	walk				
4	once a week	twice a week	every day				
5	Tesco's, post office	bank, Boots	Tesco's				
6	easy to park	nearest	nearest				

Thank you for your help

Figure 1.3

A **questionnaire** is a list of questions that you ask a number of people. Before you use a questionnaire, you need to ask yourself some questions.

- What type of questionnaire is best?
  You could go from house to house asking questions, or stand in the street, or post the questionnaire to people's houses.
- If I go to the shopping centre, which day of the week should I choose?
  People may travel further to shop at weekends and holidays and use different forms of transport.
- What time of day should I choose?
  Some times of day are busier than others.

- How many questions should I ask?
  Ask as few as you need because, generally, people do not like answering questions. Begin by explaining why you are asking the questions.
- How many people should I ask?
  Ask at least 30 people, preferably males and females of all ages.
- What questions should I ask?
  This depends upon what you want to find out.
  If you were wanting to find out the sphere of influence of a shopping centre, you might ask the questions shown in Figure 1.3.

1E PROCESSING TECHNIQUES

Once you have gathered the information you require, you need to study and analyse your findings. To do this, you need to organise your findings so they are easier to understand and use. For example, much of the information you find out can be made into tables, maps, graphs or diagrams. When you change your findings into a more useful form like this, you are using **processing techniques**. Some useful processing techniques for urban studies are now described in detail.

1F DRAWING A BAR GRAPH

A bar graph can be used to compare quantities.

- Draw an *x* axis (horizontal) and a *y* axis (vertical). Use the *y* axis to show information about quantity, for example, in Figure 1.4, the number of vehicles.
- Work out a suitable scale for the *y* axis.
- The *x* axis should be divided up equally, so that each vertical 'bar' represents one of the items you are comparing. For example, in Figure 1.4, the type of vehicle.
- Draw the axes and bars in pencil, in case you make a mistake. You can go over the lines in pen afterwards.
- Label the axes.
- Give the graph a title.

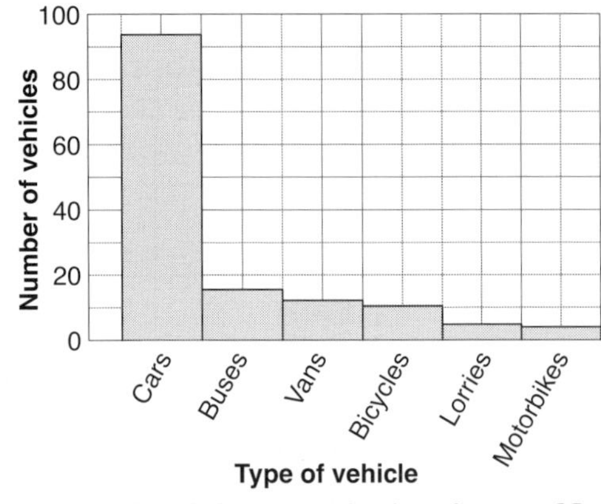

Figure 1.4 A bar graph showing traffic flow along the Dumbarton Road, 6 May 1998, 2–2.30 pm.

1G DRAWING A DIVIDED BAR GRAPH

A divided bar graph may be horizontal or vertical and is divided into sections to show different information.

- Draw the axes and choose a suitable scale for the bar graph.
- Draw in the largest section first, at the bottom (if the graph is vertical) or the left-hand side (if the graph is horizontal). For example, in Figure 1.5, the largest section is 'cars'.
- Draw the second-largest section next to the first. Work out where this section ends by adding its total to the total so far. For example, in Figure 1.5, there were 16 buses. The bus section began at 93, so it should end at 93 + 16 = 109.
- Complete all the sections.
- Draw the axes and sections in pencil first, in case you make a mistake.
- Label the axes and sections.
- Give the graph a title.

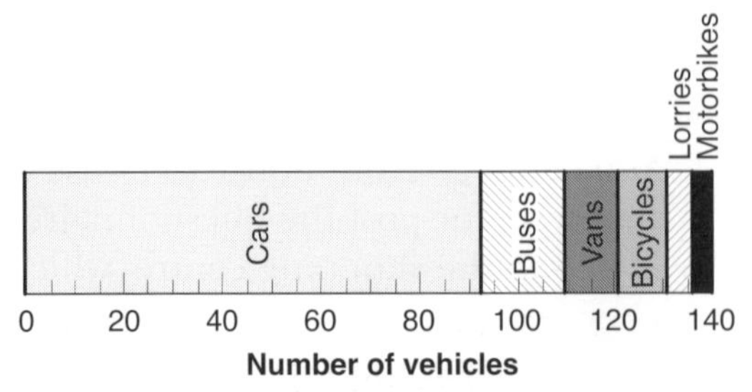

Figure 1.5 A divided bar graph showing traffic flow along the Dumbarton Road, 6 May 1998, 2–2.30 pm.

1H DRAWING A SCATTERGRAPH

A scattergraph can be used to find out if there is a relationship between two sets of figures.

- Draw an *x* and a *y* axis.
- Use the *x* axis to show information that is either a distance or time. For example, in Figure 1.6, the *x* axis represents the distance from the centre of the CBD.
- Use the *y* axis to show information about quantity or frequency. For example, in Figure 1.6, the *y* axis shows the number of pedestrians.
- Find the highest numbers you will need to show on the *x* and *y* axes and work out a suitable scale for each axis.
- Draw the axes in pencil.
- Plot each point carefully, with a small cross.
- When you have finished and have checked your graph, go over all the lines and crosses in pen.
- Label the axes.
- Give the graph a title.
- Once the scattergraph is complete, you should be able to observe the pattern and identify any trends, e.g. as one set of values increases, the other decreases.

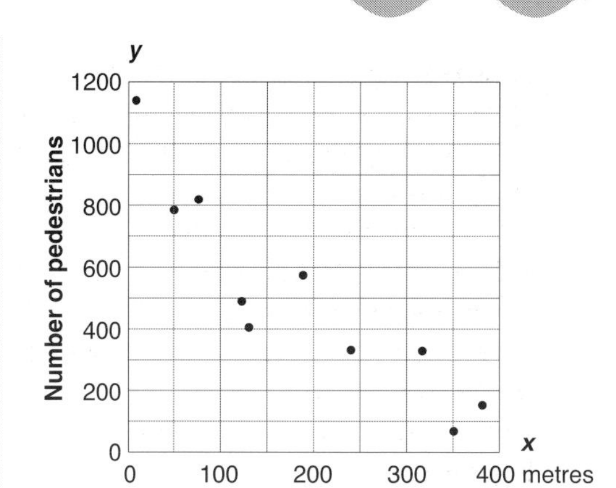

Figure 1.6 A scattergraph showing the number of pedestrians and their distance from the CBD of Inverness, 4 May 1998, 1–2 pm.

F Questions

Look at 1B.

F1 Which gathering technique would you use to find out (a) the site of a small village and (b) the different land uses in a town?

Look at 1C.

F2 You are doing a traffic survey to find out how busy a street is.
(a) Why is it a good idea to count the traffic at several places?
(b) How would you decide which day of the week to do the survey?
(c) How would you decide what time of day to do the survey?

Look at 1D.

F3 You are using a questionnaire to find out how far people travel to a shopping centre.
(a) Which would be better – to stand in the shopping centre and ask questions or to go from house to house? Give reasons for your answer.
(b) If you asked questions in the shopping centre, which day of the week would you choose? Give reasons for your answer.
(c) Why should you use your questionnaire with people of all ages?

Look at 1F.

F4 (a) Copy Figure 1.7.
(b) Complete the bar graph, using information from Figure 1.8 over the page.

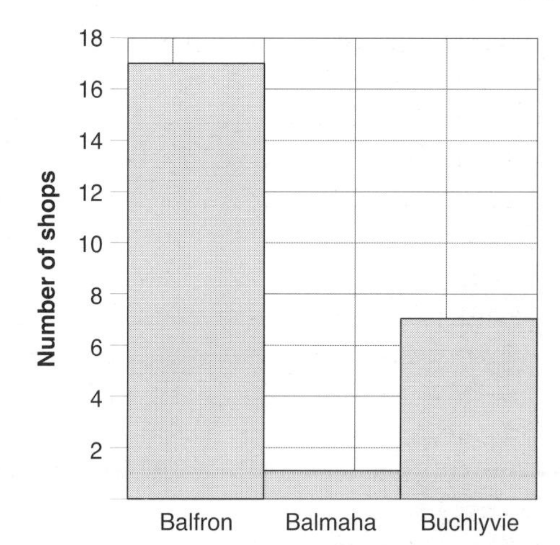

Figure 1.7 A bar graph of shops in Stirlingshire villages.

Figure 1.8

Shops in Stirlingshire villages

Village	Number of shops	Population
Balfron	17	1510
Balmaha	1	70
Buchlyvie	7	440
Croftamie	2	310
Drymen	11	820
Fintry	2	430
Killearn	10	1760
Strathblane	12	1910

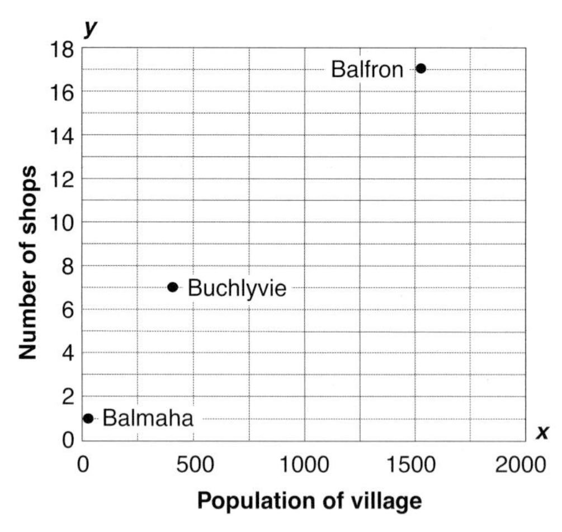

Figure 1.9 A scattergraph of the population and number of shops in Stirlingshire villages.

Look at 1H.

F5 (a) Copy Figure 1.9.
(b) Complete the scattergraph, using the information in the table above.

Look at Figures 1.10 and 1.11.

F6 Which table of information – Figure 1.10 or 1.11 – would be better shown on a bar graph?

Figure 1.10

Distance from city centre	Average price of a detached house
0.5 km	£75 000
1.0 km	£60 000
1.0 km	£50 000
1.5 km	£55 000
2.0 km	£75 000
2.5 km	£80 000
2.5 km	£100 000

Figure 1.11

Reasons for visiting a shopping centre	Number of people
Cheaper goods	5
Convenient	23
Large car park	7
Pleasant atmosphere	13

Figure 1.12

Year	Population of a village
1951	1500
1961	1900
1971	2300
1981	4700
1991	7400

Questions

Look at 1B.

G1 Which gathering technique would you use to (a) compare the housing in two areas of a town and (b) find out the site of a settlement? Give reasons for your answers.

Look at 1C.

G2 You are doing a traffic survey to compare traffic in two streets.
(a) Explain why the survey needs to be carried out at the same time in each street.
(b) Describe two other points you must consider before doing the survey and explain why they are necessary.

Look at 1D and Figure 1.13.

G3 You wish to use a questionnaire to find out how far people travel to a shopping centre.
(a) In what ways might your results be different if you stand at place X, in Figure 1.13, rather than at place Y?
(b) Describe two other things you should consider before asking people questions.
(c) Would it be better to go to people's homes and ask them questions or stand in the shopping centre? Explain your answer.

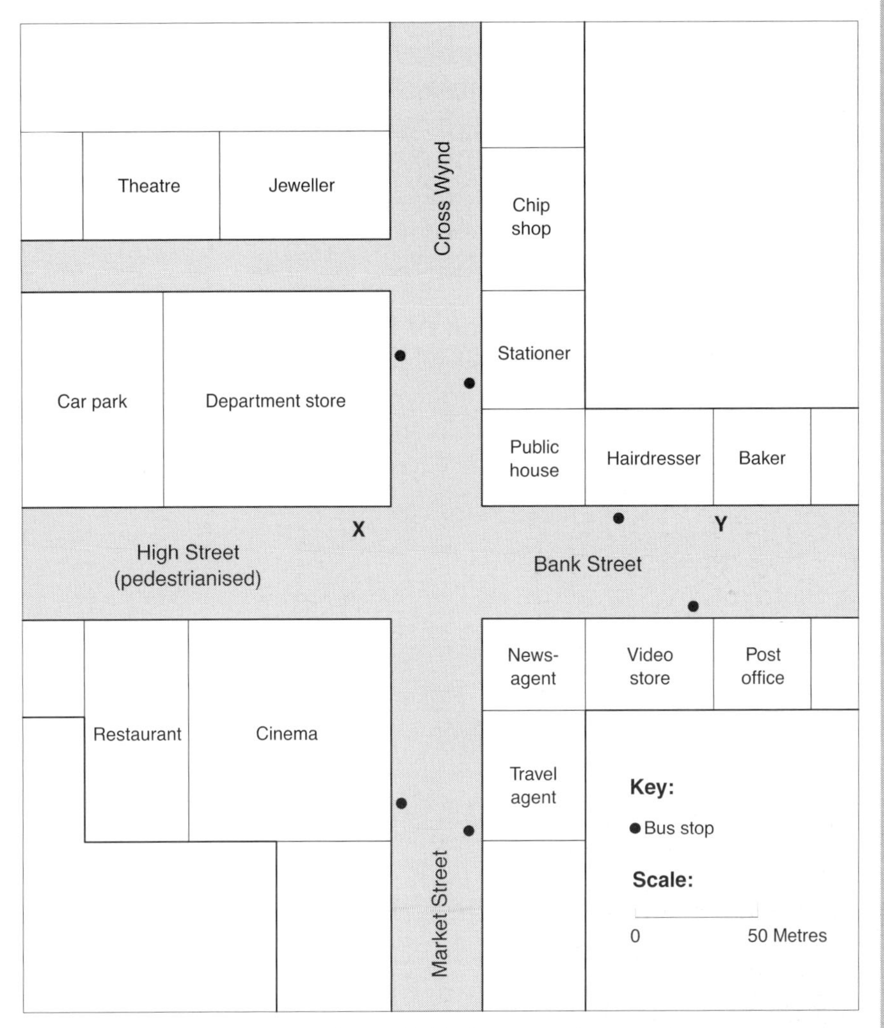

Figure 1.13 A plan of part of a town centre.

Look at 1F.

G4 Draw a bar graph using the information in the table below.

Distance travelled to shopping centre	Number of people
0–1 km	20
1–2 km	4
2–3 km	1
3–4 km	1
4–5 km	1
5 or more kilometres	3

Look at 1H.

G5 Draw a scattergraph using the information in the table below.

Distance travelled to shopping centre	Number of visits per month
10 km	4
10 km	1
7 km	10
1 km	12
5 km	6
6 km	2
2 km	10
1 km	10
4 km	8
1 km	8

Look at Figures 1.10 and 1.11.

G6 Which table of information – Figure 1.10 or 1.11 – would be better shown on a bar graph? Give a reason for your answer.

C Questions

Look at 1B.

C1 Which gathering technique would you use to find out (a) the extent of the shopping centre in a town and (b) whether a village is a commuter centre? Justify your choice of techniques.

Look at 1C.

C2 Describe how you would carry out a traffic survey to compare traffic in two streets.

Look at 1D.

C3 Compare the effectiveness of a house to house questionnaire and a street questionnaire in obtaining information about a shopping centre.

C4 (a) Describe how you would use a questionnaire to find out how far people have travelled to a shopping centre.
(b) Where, in Figure 1.13, would be the best place to stand to use your questionnaire?

Look at 1G.

C5 Draw a divided bar graph using the information in the table below.

City-centre land use	% of land used
shops	45%
offices	38%
industry	4%
public buildings	10%
housing	3%

Look at 1H.

C6 Draw a scattergraph using the information in the table below.

Land value and population density within a city

Land value (per ha.)	Population density (no. of people per km^2)
£500 000	20
£100 000	203
£25 000	57
£10 000	22
£8000	49
£50 000	123
£15 000	38

Look at Figures 1.10, 1.11 and 1.12.

C7 Which table of information – Figures 1.10, 1.11 or 1.12 – would be better shown on a scattergraph? Give a reason for your answer.

UNIT 2

The Growth and Functions of Settlements

Core text

2A SETTLEMENT SIZES

Settlements are places where people live. They are of different sizes, from the very large to the very small. The smallest are called **hamlets**. Next in size are **villages**, then **towns** and the largest are **cities**. As Figure 2.1 shows, there are more small settlements than large ones.

Scotland has settlements of all sizes, from small hamlets to large cities. Scotland's ten largest settlements are shown in the table below. They are scattered throughout Scotland, although there are more in the Central Lowlands than elsewhere. To find out why settlements developed in certain locations, we need to go back in time, because most towns and villages are several hundreds years old.

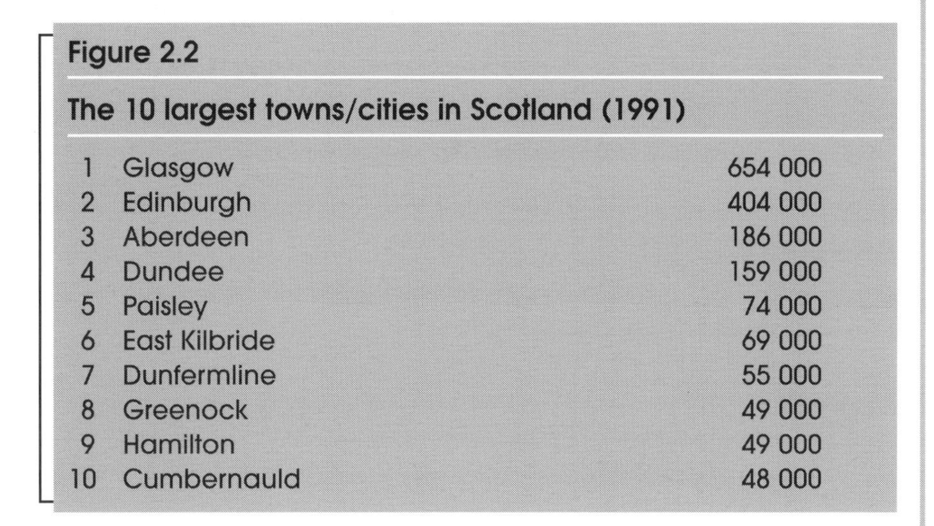

Figure 2.2

The 10 largest towns/cities in Scotland (1991)

1	Glasgow	654 000
2	Edinburgh	404 000
3	Aberdeen	186 000
4	Dundee	159 000
5	Paisley	74 000
6	East Kilbride	69 000
7	Dunfermline	55 000
8	Greenock	49 000
9	Hamilton	49 000
10	Cumbernauld	48 000

Size | Frequency
Very large | Few
City
Town
Village
Hamlet
Very small | Many

Figure 2.1 A settlement pyramid.

2B SETTLEMENT SITE

The land on which a settlement is built is called its **site**. When people first built settlements hundreds of years ago, they chose sites which provided the five things they needed most. These are shown in Figure 2.3, and are listed on the next page.

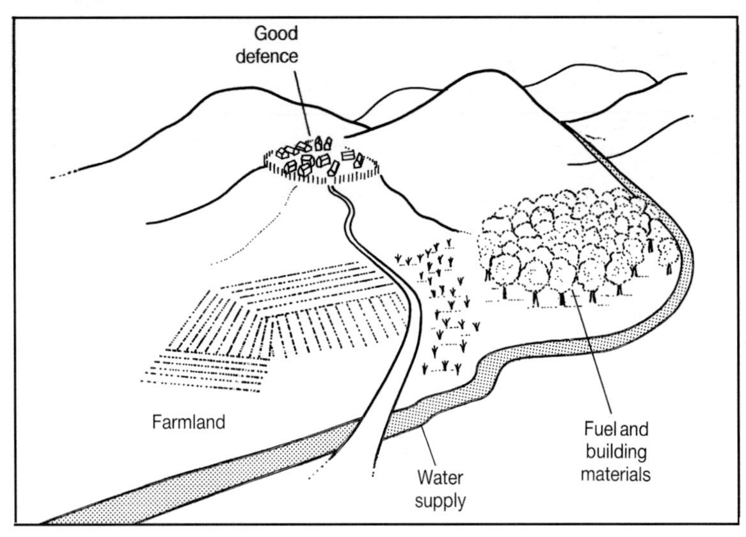

Figure 2.3 Key features of a good site for a settlement.

- **water** for drinking and washing
- **fuel**, for example, wood
- **building materials**, such as wood or stone
- **farmland** that is not too steep or marshy
- **good defence** from attackers.

Before Roman times, over 2000 years ago, many settlements were built on hilltops, because they were easy places to defend. Some of these hilltops are still settlements today, for example Edinburgh, but most have been abandoned because they were too cold and wet and there was not enough flat land for building and farming.

In later years, defence became less important, and other factors became important in choosing a site for a settlement. Some of the most common factors are shown in Figure 2.4.

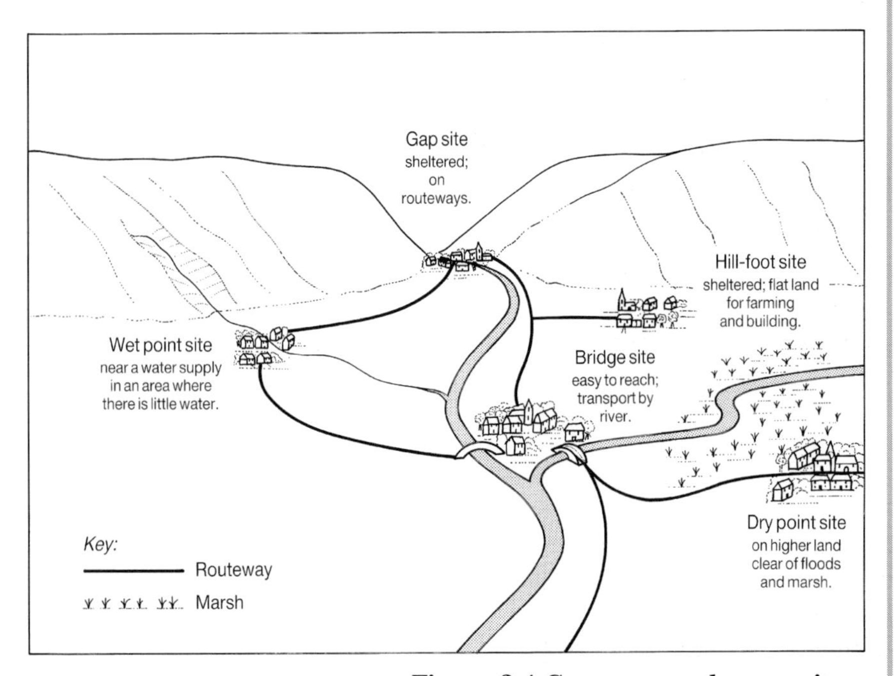

Figure 2.4 Common settlement sites.

2C THE GROWTH OF TOWNS

By about 1000 years ago, there were a large number of hamlets and villages scattered throughout Britain. Many remain small settlements today, but some have grown into towns and cities.

For a settlement to grow into a town, it had to have more **functions** and only certain places were in a suitable location to develop these functions. A settlement's functions are the activities that take place there and the smallest places have very few functions. They might provide people with a small number of services, such as a church, a shop and a public house (called a **service centre**). Bigger settlements have more functions, which is why more people choose to live in towns and cities.

Some of the first settlements in Britain to grow into towns were **market centres**. Later, **ports** and **industrial centres** grew up and, more recently, **holiday resorts** have developed.

Not only do a settlement's functions explain its growth, they also explain its characteristics – the way it looks.

2D MARKET CENTRES

A **market centre** is a settlement that has an agricultural market.

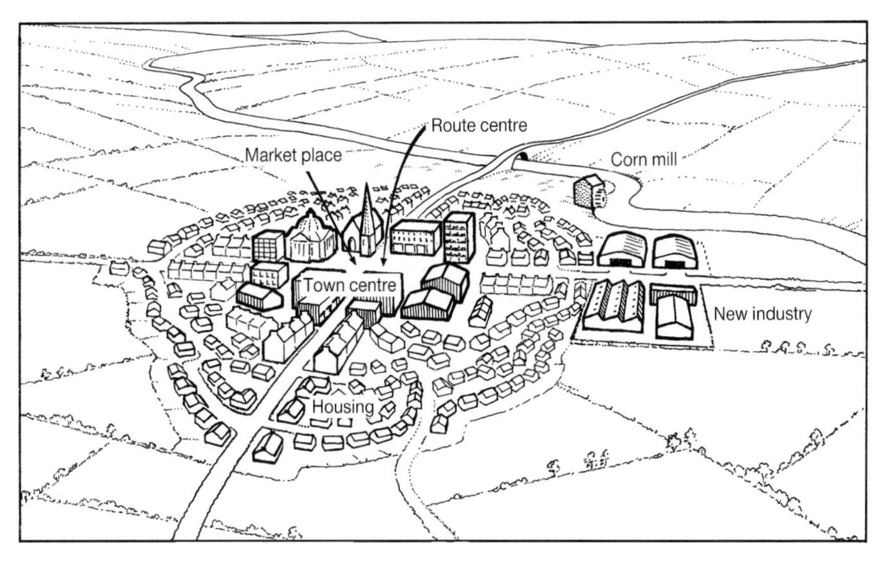

Figure 2.5 The lay-out of a typical market town.

Location:

- Market centres grew up where many routes met (**route-centres**), which were the easiest places for local people to reach.
- Places located at important bridges (**bridge sites**) and in gaps between hills (**gap sites**) often became route centres.

Dates:

- Most market centres developed between 1200 and 1800.

Characteristics:

- The market place is in the town centre, where the routes meet.
- Around the market place are agricultural industries, such as millers, seed merchants and agricultural engineers.
- Mills were often built beside the river to make use of water power.

2E INDUSTRIAL CENTRES

An **industrial centre** is a settlement in which most of the people work in factories.

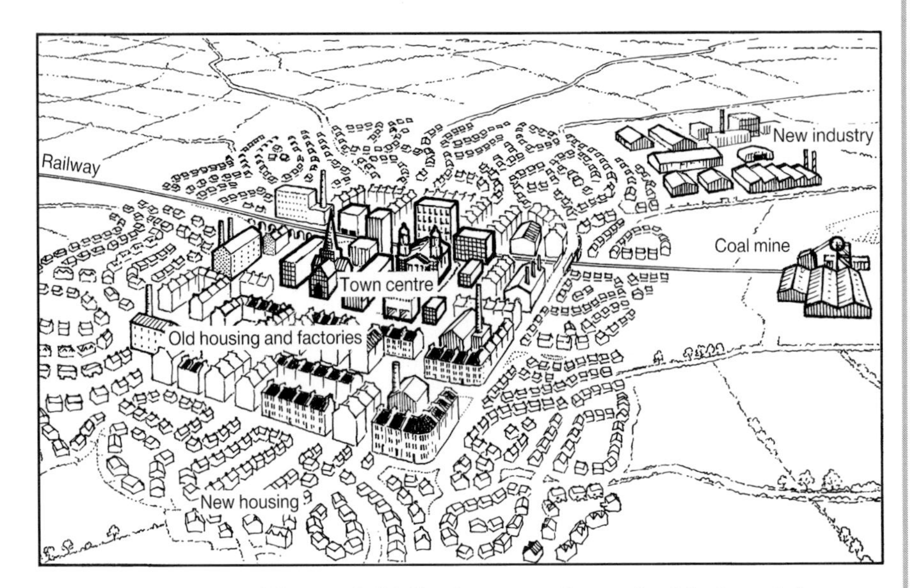

Figure 2.6 The lay-out of a typical industrial town.

Location:
- Old industrial towns were situated near sources of raw materials, especially coal, because this was the cheapest location for them.
- New industrial towns have grown up near main roads and railways.

Dates:
- Industrial centres grew rapidly from the early 1800s.

Characteristics:
- The old factories and houses, canals and railways are located near the town centre.
- New factories and businesses are built beside main roads and railways on the edge of town.

2F PORTS

A **port** is a place where goods are loaded and unloaded from ships.

Location:
- Ports grew up where there were sheltered harbours surrounded by flat land, where there were factories nearby that needed to import and export goods by ship.
- As ships became larger, ports moved to locations with deeper water.

Dates:
- Ports were important from early times, but many grew rapidly in the nineteenth century, during the Industrial Revolution.

Characteristics:
- The oldest port is usually near the town centre, with the nineteenth-century docks just downstream.

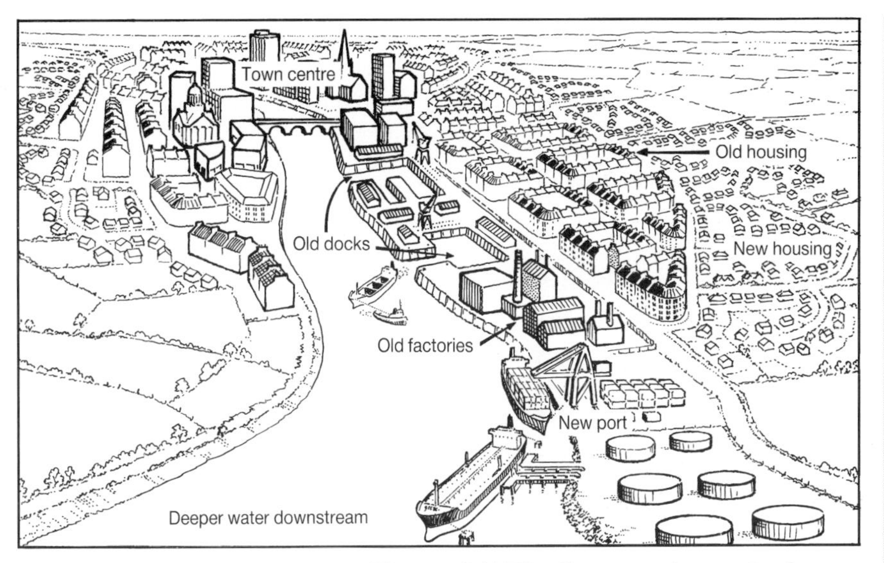

Figure 2.7 The lay-out of a typical port.

- Nineteenth-century houses and factories are close to the docks.
- The twentieth-century port is further downstream.

2G HOLIDAY RESORTS

A **holiday resort** is a settlement that is visited by many tourists.

Location:
- Resorts are found where there are attractions such as ski slopes, beaches and beautiful scenery.
- Holiday resorts need to have good communications.

Dates:
- Most holiday resorts grew from 1850 onwards.

Characteristics of coastal resorts:
- Hotels are found along the sea-front, near the town centre.
- There are many entertainments and services in the town centre.
- Housing and guest houses lie outside the town centre, where the land is cheaper.
- Camping and caravan sites and golf courses are found on the edge of town because they need a lot of space.

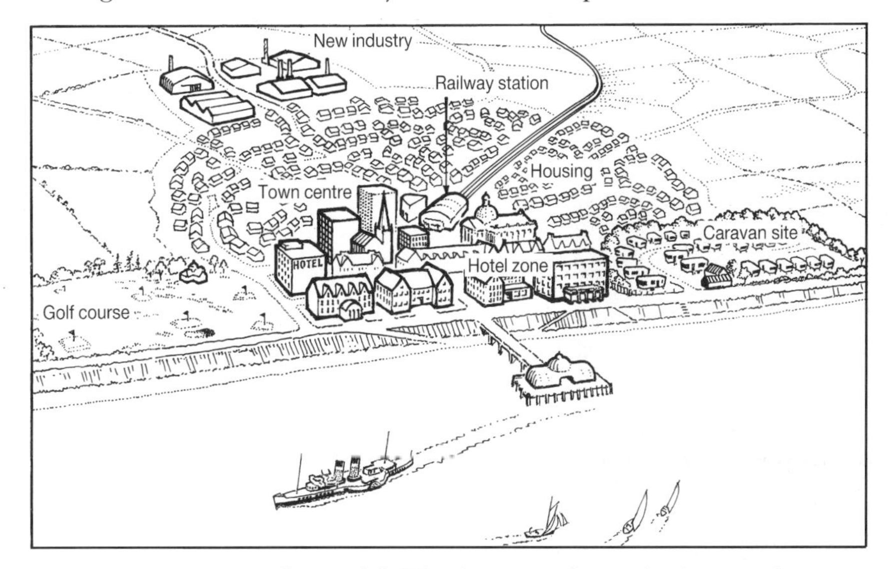

Figure 2.8 The lay-out of a typical coastal resort.

Core Questions

Look at Figure 2.1.

1 Which type of settlement – town, village, city, hamlet: (a) is the smallest, (b) is the largest, (c) occurs most often, (d) occurs least often?

Look at 2B.

2 What is meant by the 'site' of a settlement?
3 Why did early settlers need to be near trees?

Look at Figure 2.9.

4 Why do you think Durham was built on this site?

Look at 2C.

5 Give three examples of settlement functions.

Look at 2D.

6 Why did market towns grow up at route-centres?

Look at 2E.

7 What was the best location for an old industrial town?

Look at 2F.

8 What was the best location for a port?

Look at 2G.

9 Why are caravan sites not found in the centre of holiday resorts?
10 What are the main uses of buildings in the centre of holiday resorts?

Figure 2.9 The city of Durham.

F Questions

CASE STUDY OF NORTH-WEST ENGLAND

Look at Figure 2.11.

F1 What were the main reasons why people first came to live in Lancaster?

F2 Why do you think Lancaster became a market town?

F3 What other functions has Lancaster had?

Look at Figure 2.14.

F4 What are the main reasons why Liverpool became a port?

Look at Figure 2.15.

F5 Where, in Liverpool, are the old docks and the new port?

Look at Figure 2.16.

F6 Why do you think Accrington became an industrial town making cotton goods?

Look at Figure 2.17.

F7 Where, in Accrington, is the new housing and new industry?

Look at Figure 2.18.

F8 Why did Southport become an important holiday resort?

Look at Figure 2.19.

F9 What are the main land uses near the coast in Southport?

G Questions

CASE STUDY OF NORTH-WEST ENGLAND

Look at Figure 2.10.

G1 What are the main functions of the towns and cities of Lancashire?

Look at Figures 2.11 and 2.13.

G2 Describe the advantages of Lancaster as a site for early settlers.

G3 Why do you think Lancaster became a market town?

Look at Figure 2.15.

G4 (a) Describe the location of the new port in Liverpool.
(b) Is it similar to or different from the location of the new port in Figure 2.22? Give reasons for your answer.

Look at Figure 2.12.

G5 Describe the distribution of industrial towns in Lancashire.

Look at Figure 2.17.

G6 Is the location of industry in Accrington similar to its location in Figure 2.6? Give reasons for your answer.

Look at Figures 2.8 and 2.19.

G7 Describe one similarity and one difference in the coastal land uses of Southport and a typical resort.

CASE STUDY OF NORTH-WEST ENGLAND

Figure 2.10

Introduction

This is a study of settlements in the county of Lancashire and the nearby areas of Merseyside and Greater Manchester. As Figure 2.12 shows, this is mostly a lowland area, once covered with trees, and with plenty of rivers, such as the Lune, Ribble and Mersey. So, for early settlers, there were many suitable sites for settlements. Lots of hamlets and villages grew up, mainly inhabited by farmers.

Over time, some of these villages developed other functions and began to grow into towns. One of the first to grow was the Roman town of Lancaster, which gave its name to the county and became a market town. Other market towns, such as Ormskirk, also developed.

Then, in the 1800s, industrial towns sprang up, including Blackburn, Preston, Wigan and St Helens. At the same time, large ports, such as Liverpool and Manchester, began importing and exporting industrial goods.

During the last 150 years, all these towns have grown much larger. Some settlements have grown into holiday resorts, of which Blackpool, Southport and Morecambe are the best examples.

Figure 2.11

Lancaster as a Market Town

The Romans chose Lancaster as a defensive site because it is on a hilltop near a bend in the river Lune. The river provided water and the land near the river was good farmland. There were plenty of trees nearby for use as fuel and building material.

A bridge was built at the furthest point downstream that the river Lune could be bridged (called the **lowest bridging point**), and Lancaster became a route-centre. This helped it to become a market town, as well as the county town, with important services such as the sheriff court.

The river Lune at Lancaster is tidal and sheltered and, by 1700, the town had become a busy port. It also had industries, such as shipbuilding and cotton mills, but it never became an important industrial town. Lancaster's port has also declined recently, due to competition from Liverpool. Lancaster is now chiefly a service centre.

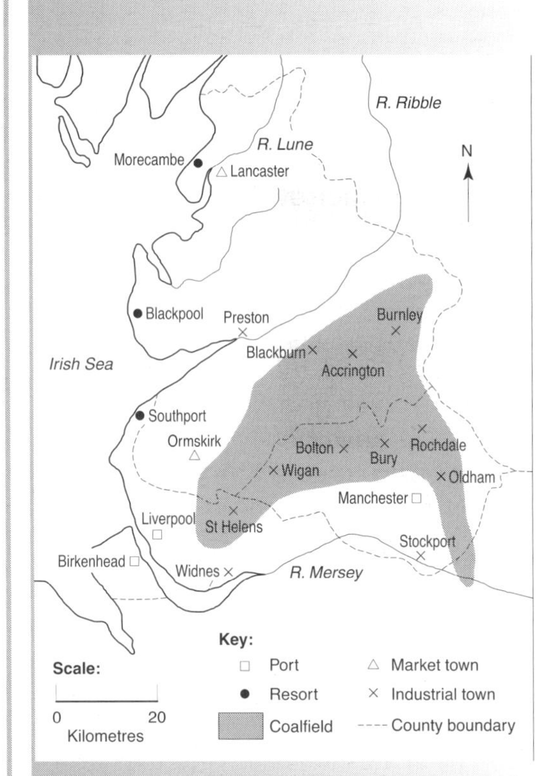

Figure 2.12 Types of settlement in north-west England.

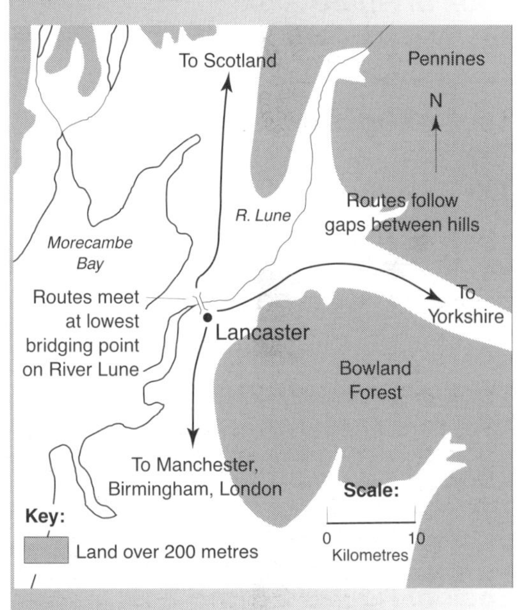

Figure 2.13 The site of Lancaster.

Figure 2.14

Liverpool as a Port

Liverpool grew up on a small hill overlooking the marshy land around the Mersey estuary. It became a small fishing port, as the Mersey was sheltered, tidal and quite deep. It did not grow into a town until 300 years ago, when it began importing goods, such as cotton needed in the industrial towns nearby. Extensive docks were dug, and canals, railways and roads were built to the port, making it easy for factories up to 100 km away to export their goods through Liverpool.

As ships have become larger in recent years, the old docks in shallow water have closed and a new port has been built in deeper water downstream. A container port has also been built downstream at Seaforth.

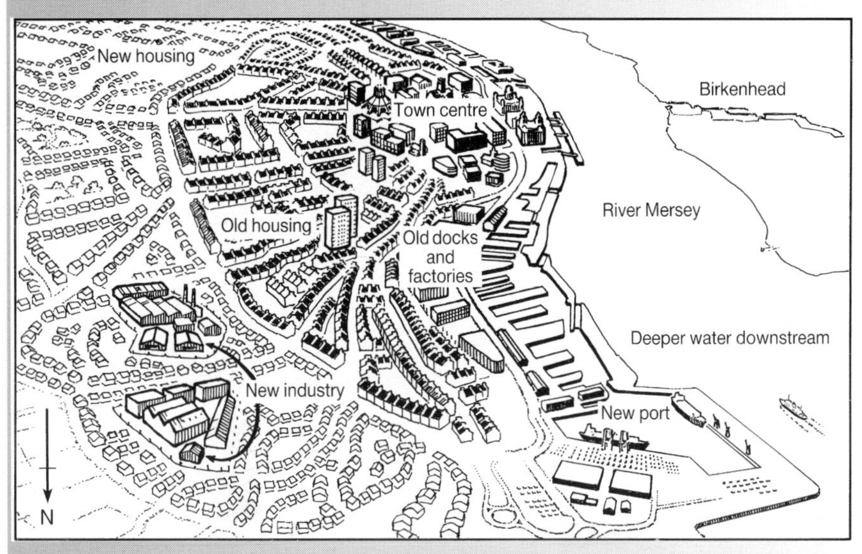

Figure 2.15 A diagram of Liverpool.

Figure 2.16

Accrington as an Industrial Town

Accrington is built on sloping land in the foothills of the Pennines. It became an industrial town in the nineteenth century and its population rose rapidly from 3000 in 1800 to 45 000 in 1900. Its main industry was cotton, for which Lancashire was world-famous. The factories at that time needed coal for power and Accrington was built on coal seams. It was also close to Liverpool, the port through which raw cotton was imported from the USA. Today, the coal mines are all closed and the cotton mills are struggling to survive in the face of competition from other countries. Very few new industries have set up in Accrington, partly because there is little suitable land on which to build. As a result, unemployment is well above the national average.

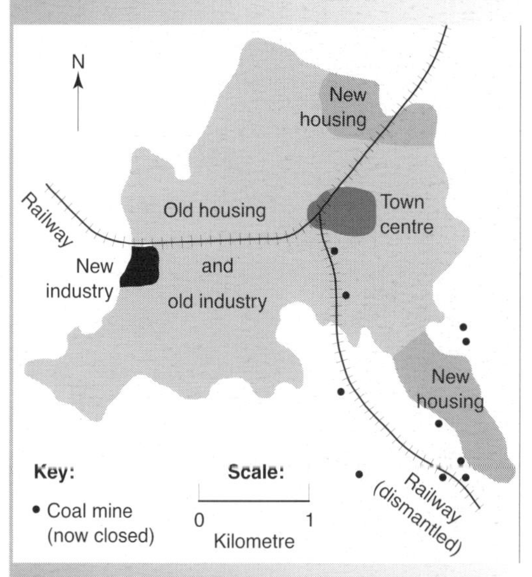

Figure 2.17 The structure of Accrington.

Figure 2.18

Southport as a Holiday Resort

Southport is not as old as most settlements in north-west England. It did not exist until 1800, when its wide, sandy beach helped it to become a small tourist resort. In 1831, a railway was built, connecting Southport to Manchester and Liverpool. Soon, thousands of people were coming to Southport for holidays. By 1850, Southport had seven times more visitors than the popular resort of Blackpool.

Southport did not develop many other functions, although it has recently become a retirement centre. Its attractive, quiet location away from polluted industrial areas has made it a popular choice for people to move to when they retire.

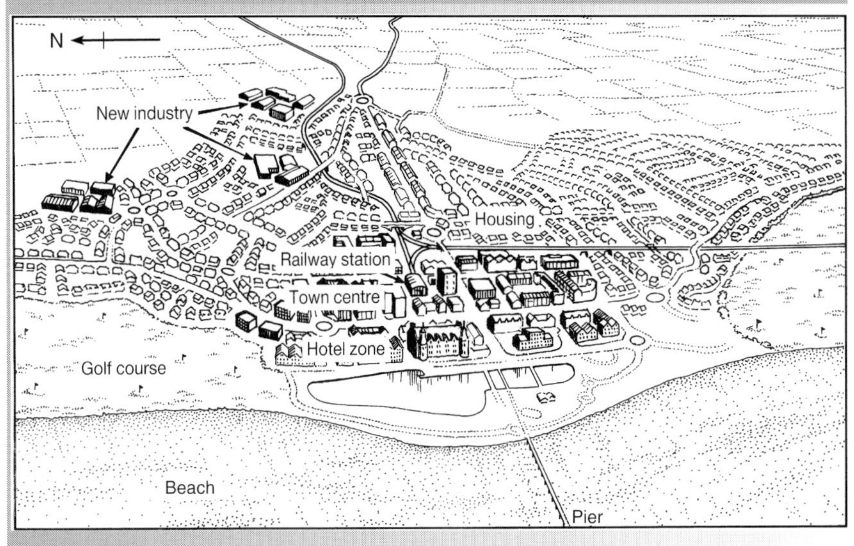

Figure 2.19 A diagram of Southport.

Figure 2.20 Lancaster.

Figure 2.21 Liverpool's port in 1920.

Figure 2.22 Old mills in Accrington.

Figure 2.23 Southport beach.

Extension Text

2H GEOGRAPHICAL MODELS OF SETTLEMENTS

Geographical models simplify the features found in settlements. They show only the main features that most settlements of a particular type possess. This makes it easier to analyse the characteristics of different settlement types. Models are usually drawn in plan form. Three such models are shown in Figures 2.24, 2.25 and 2.26. They are plan views of the sketches in Figures 2.5, 2.7 and 2.8.

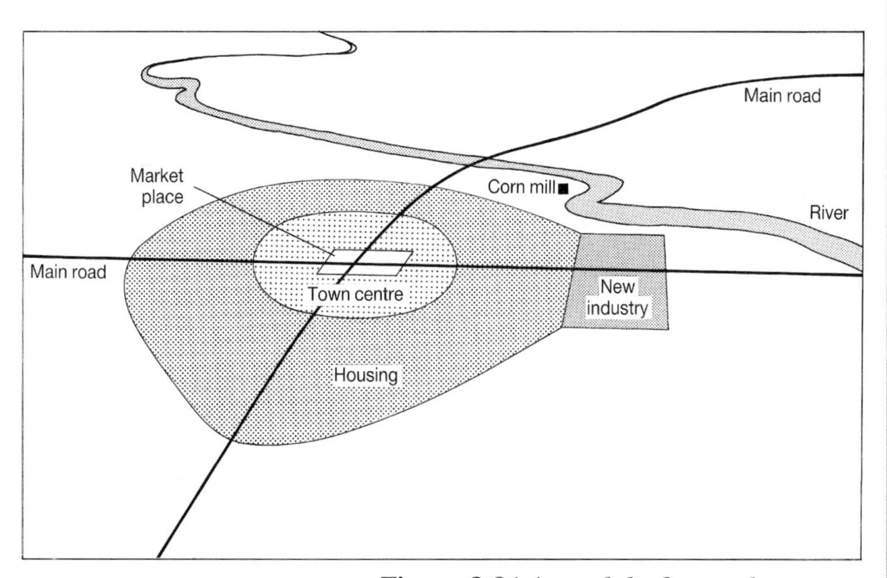

Figure 2.24 A model of a market town.

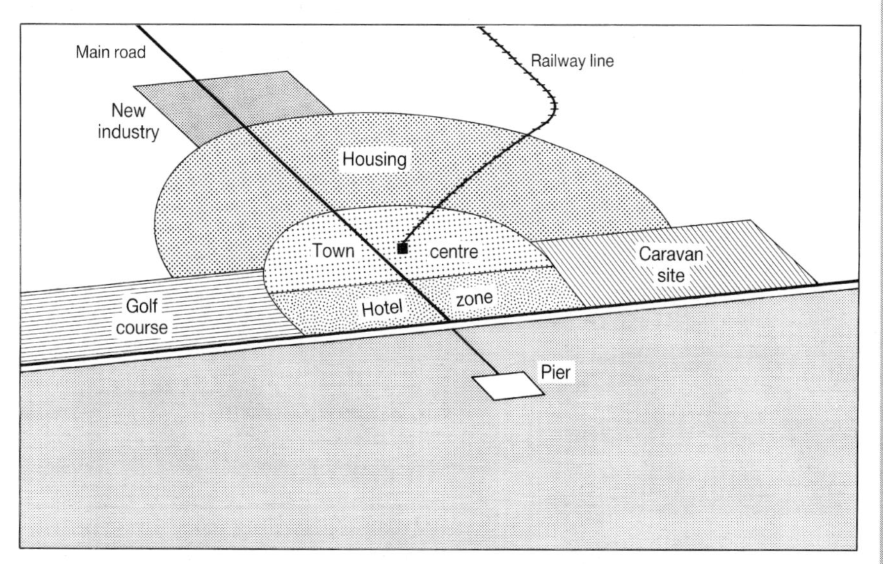

Figure 2.25 A model of a coastal resort.

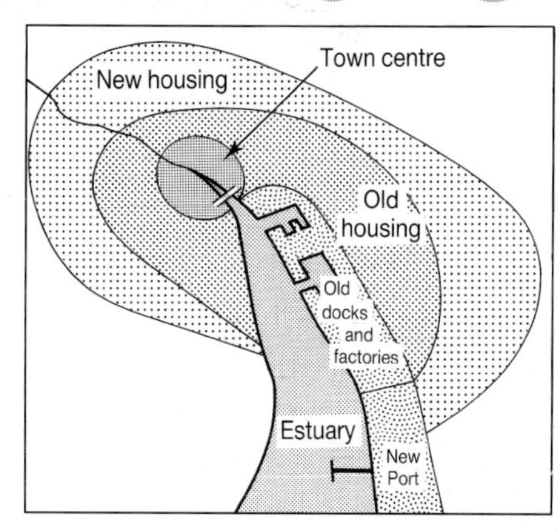

Figure 2.26 A model of a port.

2I SETTLEMENT PATTERNS

The settlement pattern describes the distribution or spread of settlements in an area. The pattern may be one of three types:

- **Nucleated** – the buildings are grouped together, for example, in villages or small towns. This grouping may occur for defensive or social reasons. It also allows services to develop, such as churches, public houses and general stores.

- **Dispersed** – the buildings are scattered. In farming areas, farmhouses are often in the middle of their fields, making it easier and quicker for the farmer to reach each field.
- **Composite** – there is a mixture of dispersed and nucleated patterns.

Extension Questions

Read the Extension Text.

E1 What are the advantages of (a) a nucleated and (b) a dispersed settlement pattern?
E2 In what ways is a geographical model of a settlement different from a real settlement?
E3 Draw a plan of a model industrial town, based on Figure 2.6.
E4 Explain the land-use pattern of a typical industrial town.
E5 Explain the land-use pattern of a typical market town.

C Questions

Look at Figures 2.11 and 2.13.

C1 In what ways did the site of Lancaster encourage the settlement to grow?

Look at Figures 2.14 and 2.15.

C2 Describe the advantages and disadvantages of Liverpool's site.
C3 Compare the land-use pattern of Liverpool with the plan of a model port in Figure 2.7.

Look at Figures 2.16 and 2.17.

C4 Do you think the layout of Accrington is typical of that of an industrial town? Give reasons for your answer.

Look at Figure 2.19.

C5 Describe the relationship between land use and distance from the sea-front in Southport.

UNIT 3

Settlements as Service Centres

Core Text

3A TYPES OF SERVICES

In Unit 2 we looked at the different functions of settlements. An important function of settlements is to provide **services** for the people who live there, such as schools, hospitals and shops. Settlements which provide services are called **service centres**.

Low-order services are services that are used very often so there are a great many of them, for example, post offices and public houses. They are found in settlements of all sizes. **Middle-order services** are services that are used quite often, so there are quite a lot of them, for example, hairdressers and chemists. They are found in towns and cities. **High-order services** are services that are not used very often, so there are very few of them, for example, sports stadiums and furniture shops. They are found in cities.

3B SPHERE OF INFLUENCE

The **sphere of influence** of a service is the area from which its customers come. Figure 3.1 shows the spheres of influence of three services in Stirling. High-order services, such as department stores, have large spheres of influence. People are willing to travel long

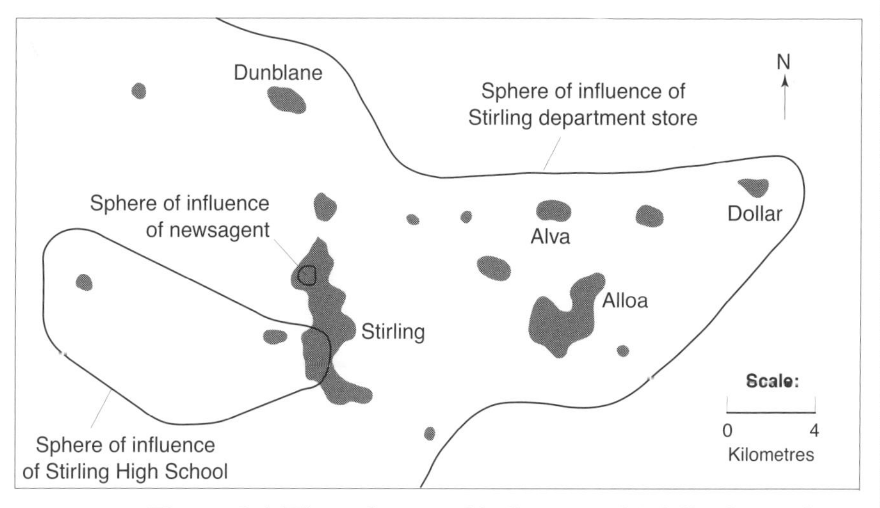

Figure 3.1 The spheres of influence of Stirling's services.

distances to them because (a) there are so few of these services, and (b) they do not visit them very often. Low-order services, such as newsagents, have small spheres of influence. People are only willing to travel short distances to them because (a) they need to visit them often, and (b) there are lots of them.

3C THE SPHERE OF INFLUENCE OF A SETTLEMENT

The sphere of influence of a settlement is the area from which people come to use the services of that settlement.

Figure 3.2 shows the sphere of influence of three settlements on the Isle of Lewis and Harris in the Outer Hebrides. Towns, such as Stornoway, and cities have large spheres of influence. People are willing to travel long distances to use their services because (a) they provide middle- and high-order services, and (b) they have good communications, making them easy to reach. Villages and hamlets, such as Tarbert and Kyles, have small spheres of influence. People only travel short distances to use their services because (a) they only have low-order services, and (b) they do not usually have good communications.

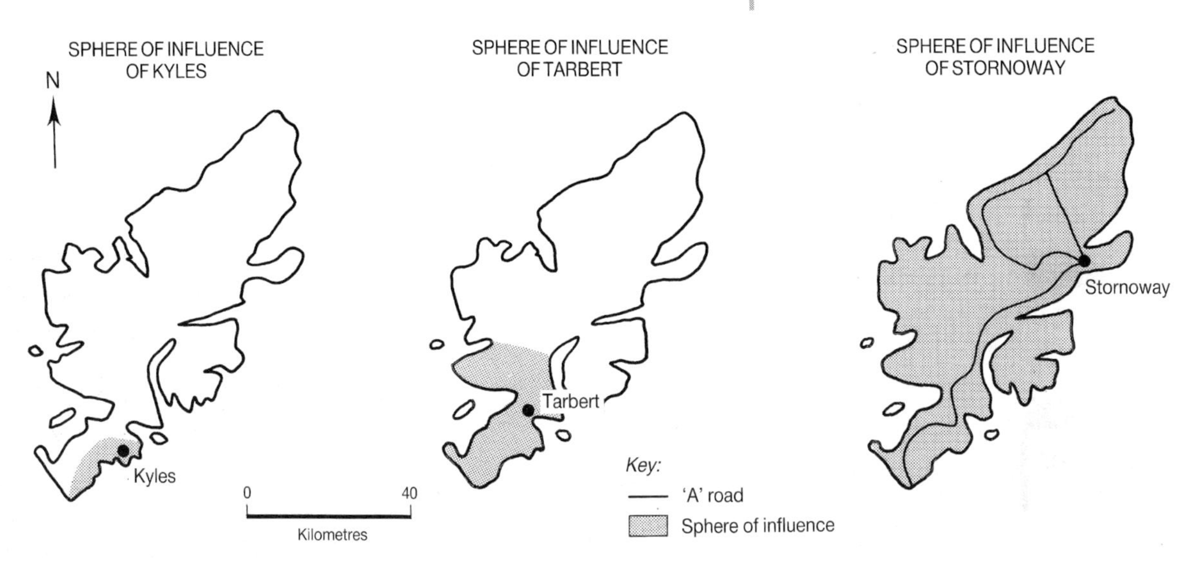

Figure 3.2 The spheres of influence of settlements on the Isle of Lewis and Harris.

3D SETTLEMENTS AND SERVICES

People usually go to the nearest settlement that provides the services they want to use. The people of Kyles on the Isle of Harris use the post office in Kyles. They go to Tarbert to use the bank and to Stornoway to buy furniture. But people do not always go to the nearest settlement. There are other factors which may affect which service they use. These are shown in Figure 3.3.

3E OTHER NAMES FOR SPHERES OF INFLUENCE

Spheres of influence are sometimes given other names. The sphere of influence of a shop, for example, is often called its **trade area** or **market area**. The sphere of influence of a school is usually called its **catchment area**. The sphere of influence of a port is called its **hinterland**. The hinterland is the area containing the factories which use that port to import and export their goods.

Figure 3.3 Reasons for choosing service centres.

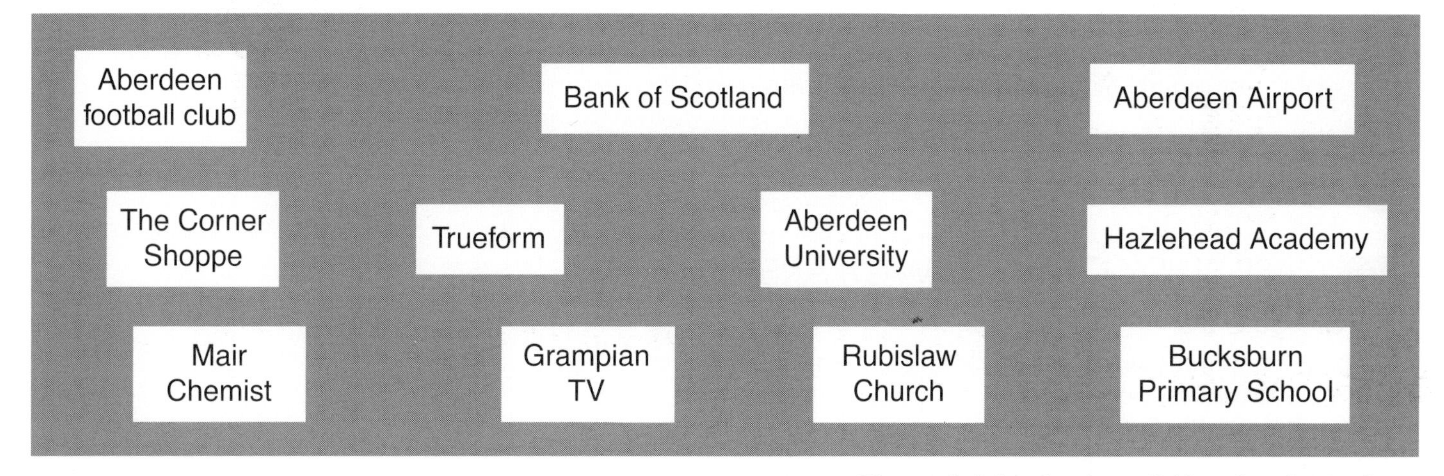

Figure 3.4 A selection of Aberdeen's services.

Core Questions

Look at 3A.

1 Which of Aberdeen's services, shown in Figure 3.4, are (a) low-order, (b) middle-order, (c) high-order?

2 Are the following statements true or false?
   (a) Middle-order services are more common than low-order services.
   (b) High-order services are often found in villages.
   (c) High-order services are used less often than middle-order services.

Look at 3B.

(d) The sphere of influence of a jeweller is the area where its customers come from.

(e) High-order services have large spheres of influence.

Look at 3C.

(f) Hamlets have a large sphere of influence.

Look at 3D.

(g) People always go to the nearest settlement for their services.

Look at 3E.

(h) A school's catchment area is where its pupils come from.

(i) The area served by a port is called its hinterland.

3 Choose the two correct endings for each statement below.

(a) Department stores have larger spheres of influence than newsagents because:
- (i) they sell more expensive goods.
- (ii) it is easier to park nearby.
- (iii) they sell goods used every day.
- (iv) they are not found in every town or village.

(b) The sphere of influence of a town might be increased by:
- (i) an increase in the town's population.
- (ii) the building of a new covered shopping precinct.
- (iii) the opening of more newsagents.
- (iv) the improvement of the roads to the town.

(c) There are more newsagents than jewellers in Scotland because:
- (i) jewellers are used more often.
- (ii) newsagents are used more often.
- (iii) people will travel further to a jeweller.
- (iv) newsagents have a larger sphere of influence.

F Questions

CASE STUDY OF THE HAWICK AREA

Look at Figure 3.5.

F1 Which two settlements in the Hawick area have:
- (a) the greatest populations;
- (b) the smallest populations;
- (c) the most services;
- (d) the fewest services?

Look at Figure 3.8.

F2 Compare the number of post offices and shoe shops in the Hawick area?

F3 Suggest why there are more shoe shops than furniture shops.

F4 Why do you think there is no shoe shop in the village of Denholm?

F5 The people from which villages use the post office in Hawick?

F6 Which do you think will be bigger – the sphere of influence of Hawick's post office or its shoe shop? Give reasons for your answer.

Figure 3.5 Shops in the Hawick area

Settlement	Population	Number of shops	Order of shops
Hawick	15 719	175	low, middle, high
Galashiels	13 766	158	low, middle, high
Selkirk	5952	77	low, middle
Jedburgh	4088	75	low, middle
Melrose	2276	40	low, middle
St. Boswell's	1143	14	low, middle
Newtown	1116	3	low
Denholm	593	4	low, high
Ancrum	355	1	low
Bowden	246	1	low
Lilliesleaf	225	3	low
Bonchester	141	1	low
Midlem	96	0	
Ashkirk	96	0	
Lanton	80	0	
Ettrickbridge	70	0	
Chesters	56	0	
Minto	46	0	
Roberton	39	0	
Teviothead	28	1	middle

Look at Figure 3.9.

F7 In what ways do shops in the suburbs of Hawick differ from those in the centre?

Look at Figures 3.11 and 3.14.

F8 Do you think Edinburgh's shopping centre attracts many people from the Hawick area? Give reasons for your answer.

Figure 3.6 Hawick's main shopping street.

G Questions

CASE STUDY OF THE HAWICK AREA

Look at Figure 3.5.

G1 In the Hawick area, is there a connection between:
(a) the population of a settlement and the number of shops there;
(b) the population of a settlement and the order of shops found there? Give reasons for each answer.

Look at Figure 3.8.

G2 (a) Compare the number of post offices, shoe shops and furniture shops in this area.
(b) Suggest reasons for the different numbers.

G3 Suggest reasons for the sphere of influence of Hawick's post office.

G4 Why do you think there is no Marks and Spencer in this area?

G5 Describe the likely sphere of influence of Jedburgh's shoe shops.

Look at Figure 3.9.

G6 Why are the shops in the suburbs of Hawick different from those in the centre?

Look at Figures 3.11 and 3.12.

G7 Which city do you think most people in Hawick visit for high-order services – Edinburgh or Carlisle? Give reasons for your answer.

CASE STUDY OF THE HAWICK AREA

Figure 3.7

Introduction

This area is in the Scottish Borders close to England. It is made up of five towns (Hawick, Galashiels, Jedburgh, Selkirk and Melrose) and a greater number of hamlets and villages. The towns are all industrial towns, having grown up as a result of the woollen industry. World-famous companies, such as Pringle, still make high-quality knitwear here. Some of the towns are also market centres, serving the needs of the large farming population who live and work in this area.

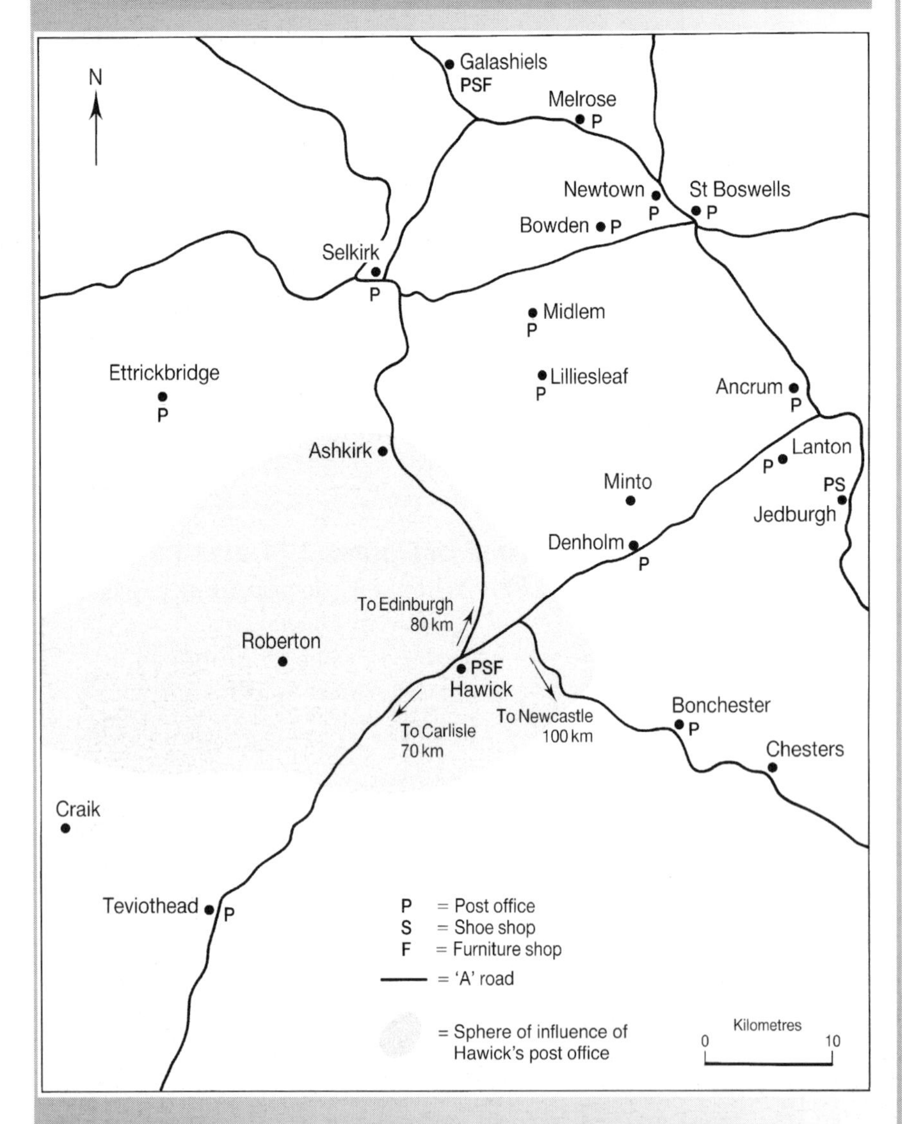

Figure 3.8 The locations of three types of shop in the Hawick area.

Figure 3.9

The Location of Services

Figure 3.8 shows the location of the settlements in the Hawick area. They range from the tiniest hamlets to small towns and they are all service centres. Figure 3.5 shows the number and order of services that they provide. They are mostly low- and middle-order services. The towns are not large enough for many high-order services, such as department stores, to make a profit. Hawick and Galashiels are the only settlements in the area large enough to have suburban shops as well as town centre shops. The suburban shops are few and are only low-order services, such as newsagents and fish and chip shops. This is because they are not easy to reach, except by the people living in the housing areas nearby.

Figure 3.10

The Sphere of Influence of the Settlements

Hawick and Galashiels have the greatest spheres of influence because they have the highest order services in the area, such as furniture shops and car showrooms. The villages have smaller spheres of influence because they only have low-order services, such as general stores and post offices. Generally, the people go to the nearest settlement for their services. In some cases, however, they go to the settlement which is quickest to reach. This may not be the nearest, as it depends on how good the road connections are. In addition, many people use the services in the place in which they work, rather than the place in which they live.

Figure 3.11

The Attractions of Edinburgh

The nearest settlements which provide many high-order services, such as Marks and Spencer, for the people of this area are Edinburgh and Carlisle.

Edinburgh is 80 km from Hawick. It has a wide range of shops, some very high-order shops and plenty of choice. Some of the shops are in covered precincts, but they are spread over a wide area. There are, in addition, many cultural and historical attractions in Edinburgh. This can make it very crowded, especially in summer. The roads are congested and it can be very difficult to park.

Figure 3.12

The Attractions of Carlisle

Carlisle is 70 km from Hawick and is not as congested as Edinburgh, nor is it as difficult to park. It has many high-order services, but not as many as Edinburgh, although the largest ones advertise on local television. Carlisle has a covered shopping area and some of its streets are pedestrianised.

Figure 3.13 The Lanes shopping area, Carlisle.

Figure 3.14 The Waverley Shopping Centre, Edinburgh.

Extension Text

3F A SETTLEMENT HIERARCHY

In any area, the settlements form a **hierarchy**. This means that they can be put into order, according to how important they are (e.g. how many people live there, how many services there are, how high is the order of services they have). As with any hierarchy, there are usually more at the bottom than there are at the top.

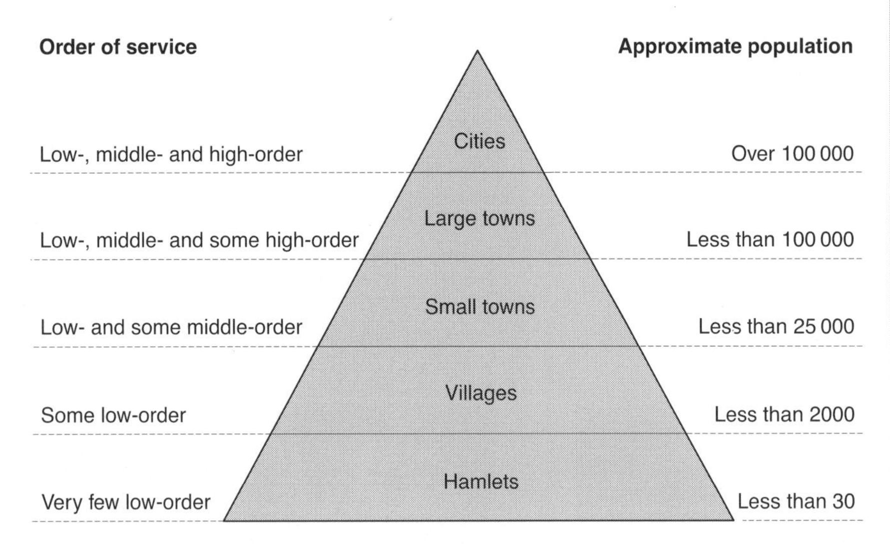

Figure 3.15 A settlement hierarchy.

3G RANGE AND THRESHOLD

Low-order services are found in settlements of every size, whereas high-order services are only found in large towns and cities. This is because people are not prepared to travel far to services they use often. The maximum distance people will travel to a service is called its **range distance**. A low-order service has a small range. A high-order service has a large range.

High-order services are only found in large towns and cities because, as most people do not use them very often, they need a large population living nearby. The minimum number of people living nearby for a service to make a profit is called its **threshold population**. A high-order service has a large threshold population. A low-order service has a small threshold population.

For a service to exist in any settlement, its threshold population must live within the range distance. For example, a chemist shop needs 10 000 people living within 8 km. A large department store needs 100 000 people living within 40 km.

E Questions

Read 3F and 3G.

E1 Describe the settlement hierarchy in the area in which you live.

E2 What is meant by the terms 'threshold population' and 'range distance'.

E3 Why does a low-order service have a small threshold population?

E4 Why does a high-order service have a large range distance?

E5 How is it possible for a large department store, needing a threshold population of 100 000 people, to make a profit in a town of only 70 000 people?

C Questions

CASE STUDY OF THE HAWICK AREA

Look at Figure 3.5.

C1 In the Hawick area, what is the relationship between a settlement's population, its number of shops and its order of shops?

Look at Figure 3.8.

C2 What is the approximate range distance of (a) a post office and (b) a shoe shop in the area?

C3 What is the approximate threshold population of a shoe shop?

C4 Suggest reasons why the sphere of influence of Hawick's furniture shop is greater than that of its own shoe shops.

Look at Figures 3.11 and 3.12.

C5 Describe the different points of view that the people of Hawick might have towards using Edinburgh and Carlisle for high-order services.

UNIT 4

Land Uses in Towns

Core Text

4A LAND-USE ZONES

Nearly all towns and cities have areas of old housing and new housing called **housing zones**, areas of old factories and new factories called **industrial zones**, and areas of shops and offices called **business districts**. These areas are the main **land-use zones** in a town.

Figure 4.1 Land-use zones in a town.

Land-use zones are found in similar locations in most towns. The **central business district** (**CBD**) or town centre is usually found where the main roads meet. Next to the CBD are the old industrial and old housing zones. These were built in the nineteenth century at the edge of the town, as it then was. Together, the CBD and the old housing and old industrial zones make up the **inner city**.

The new housing, new industry and new business districts are found in the outskirts or **suburbs**, where there is more space for building. These land-use zones all have different characteristics.

4B THE CENTRAL BUSINESS DISTRICT

The CBD usually has:

- high-order shops
- main roads meeting
- offices, hotels and entertainment
- the Town Hall, the main bus and railway stations
- the heaviest traffic
- the oldest part of town, with many churches and narrow roads
- the most expensive land, and thus the tallest and the most densely-packed buildings.

4C THE OLD INDUSTRIAL ZONE

The old industrial zone usually has:

- tall factories built of brick or stone
- factories with chimneys
- some waste land, where old factories have been pulled down
- some new industries replacing the old factories
- nearby railways and canals
- little greenery
- quite heavy traffic
- densely-packed buildings
- buildings with slate roofs.

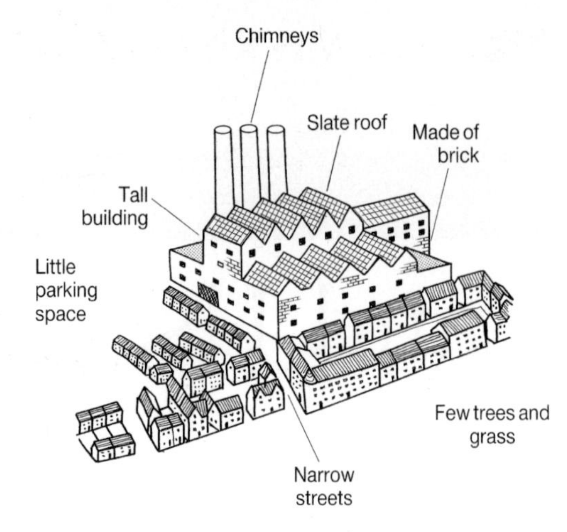

Figure 4.2 An old industrial zone.

4D THE OLD HOUSING ZONE

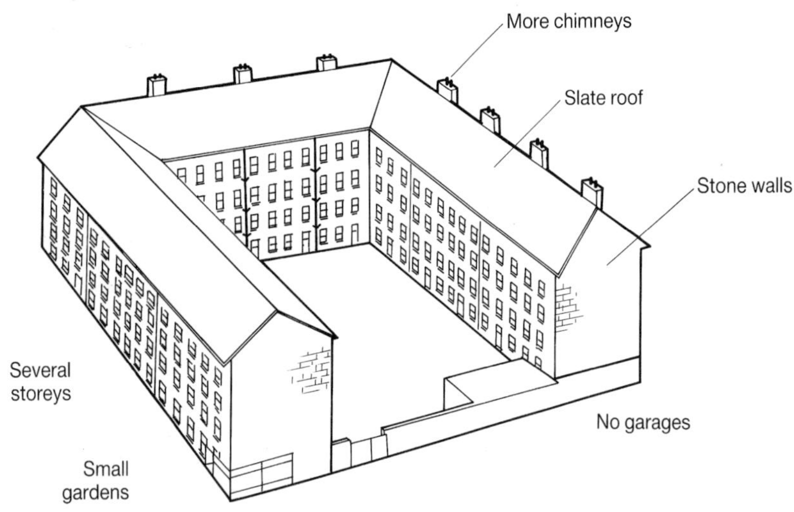

Figure 4.3 An old housing zone.

The old housing zone usually has:

- two- or three-storey **terraced** houses, or four or five storey **tenement** blocks
- houses with many chimneys
- little greenery
- straight streets at 90° to each other (a **grid-iron pattern**)
- densely-packed buildings
- factories nearby, within walking distance of old housing
- buildings built of stone, with slate roofs
- some old housing replaced by new housing, such as high-rise flats
- some old housing, which is detached and of lower density.

4E THE NEW HOUSING ZONE

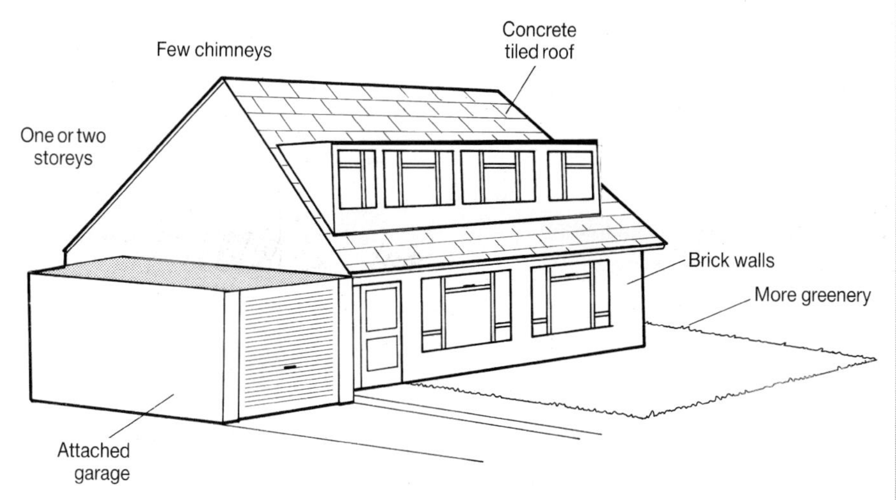

Figure 4.4 A typical house in a new housing zone.

The new housing zone usually has:
- one- or two-storey detached and semi-detached houses
- some blocks of high-rise flats
- houses with larger gardens
- parks nearby
- streets in the shape of crescents, squares or cul-de-sacs (dead-ends)
- low-order services
- houses built of brick, with tile roofs
- little traffic.

4F THE NEW INDUSTRIAL ZONE

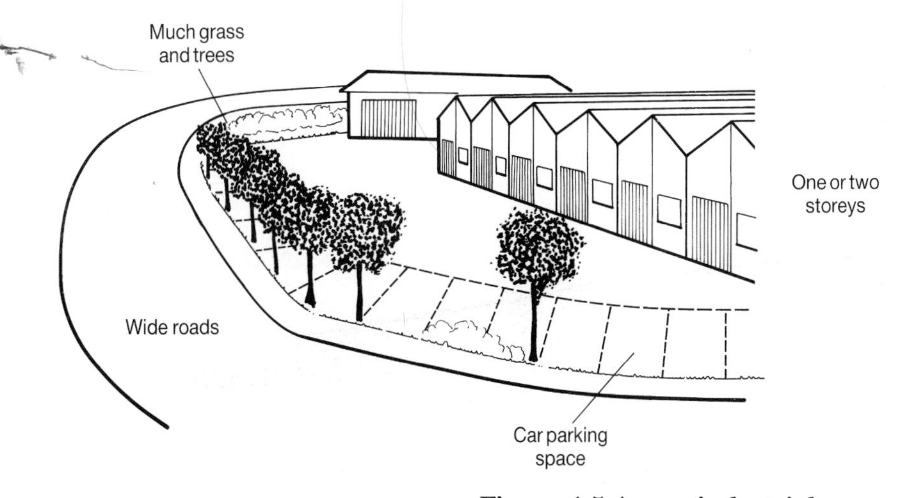

Figure 4.5 A new industrial zone.

The new industrial zone usually:
- has one- or two-storey buildings
- is in a planned industrial estate
- is away from housing
- is landscaped with grass and trees
- is beside main roads
- has plenty of parking spaces
- has buildings built of brick, with few chimneys
- has cheap land, with room to expand.

4G THE NEW BUSINESS DISTRICT

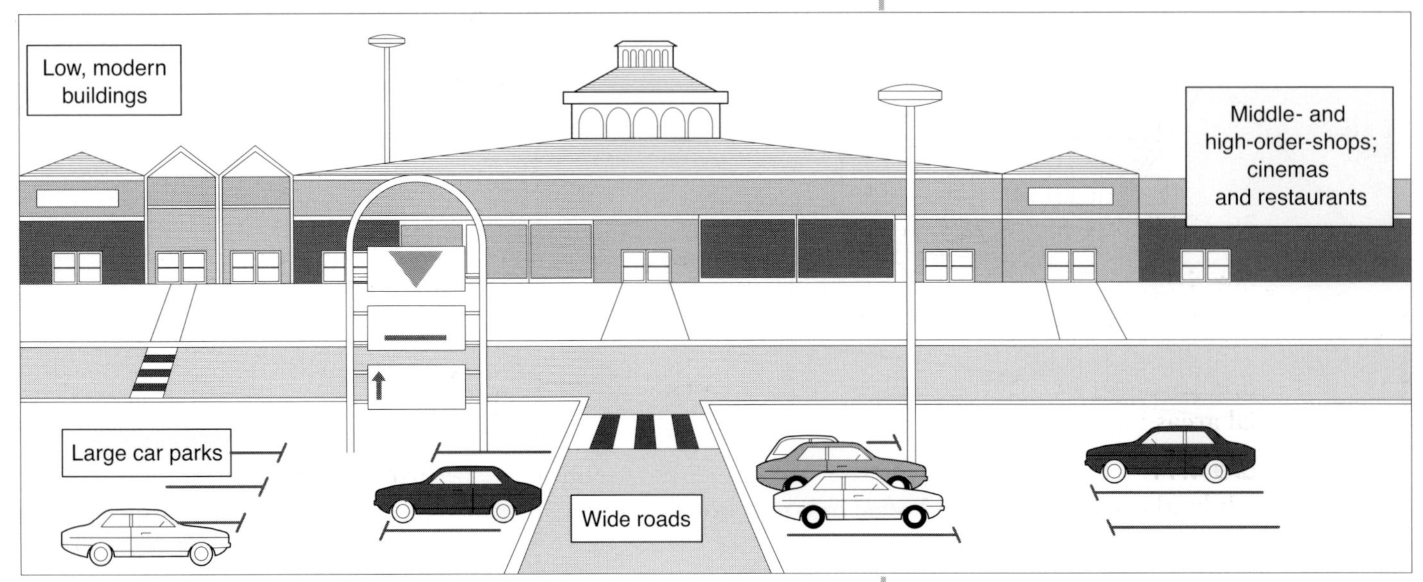

Figure 4.6 A new business district.

The new business district usually:

- has high-order shops, such as large supermarkets and electrical stores
- has other services, such as restaurants, cinemas and bowling alleys
- is separate from housing and industry
- is landscaped with grass
- is beside main roads, often where main roads meet
- has plenty of parking spaces
- has cheap land, with room to expand
- is in a planned retail park.

Core Questions

Look at 4A.

1 Where in a town would you find the CBD?
2 Which three land-use zones make up the inner city?

Look at 4B.

3 Why are many roads narrow in the CBD?
4 Why are the tallest buildings usually found in the CBD?

Look at 4D.

5 Why do you think houses were built close to factories in the nineteenth century?
6 Which land-use zones are shown in Figure 4.7? Give reasons for your answer.

Look at 4A–4F.

7 In which zone – CBD, old housing zone, old industrial zone, new housing zone, new industrial zone – would you expect to find: (a) the Town Hall, (b) tall factories, (c) blocks of flats, (d) tenement blocks, (e) shops, (f) streets in crescents, (g) industrial estates, (h) the tallest buildings, (i) the heaviest traffic, and (j) the railway station?

Figure 4.7

Look at 4G.

8 Why are new shopping centres often built on the outskirts of towns?

F Questions

CASE STUDY OF GLASGOW

Look at Figure 4.10.

F1 Which land-use zone in Glasgow has (a) the largest area and (b) the smallest area?

F2 Where are (a) the old industrial areas and (b) the new industrial areas in Glasgow found?

Look at Figure 4.11.

F3 (a) Which land-use zone has the highest population density? (b) Why do you think the population is so high in this area?

Look at Figure 4.12.

F4 What is the value of land in the centre of Glasgow?

Look at Figure 4.8.

F5 How do you know that this photograph shows Glasgow's CBD?

F6 Describe the main features of the housing in Figure 4.13.

F7 How do you know that the housing in Figure 4.15 is quite new?

Look at Figure 4.16.

F8 Describe the advantages of this location for a new retail park.

Figure 4.8 Glasgow city centre.

G Questions

CASE STUDY OF GLASGOW

Look at Figure 4.10.

G1 Describe the location of the old housing areas in Glasgow.

G2 Compare the locations of the old and new industrial areas.

Look at Figure 4.12.

G3 Describe the changes in land value from Glasgow city centre to its northern boundary.

G4 Why do you think the population density is so low in the centre of Glasgow?

Look at Figure 4.8.

G5 What evidence is there that this photograph shows the centre of Glasgow?

G6 Describe the main characteristics of the housing in Figure 4.15.

G7 What evidence is there that the housing in Figure 4.13 is old, low-cost housing?

Look at Figure 4.16.

G8 Do you think this is a suitable location for a retail park? Give reasons for your answer.

CASE STUDY OF GLASGOW

Figure 4.9

Introduction

Glasgow was first settled on the north side of the Clyde, between the river and the present-day cathedral. It grew slowly at first, mostly as a market centre for local farmers. In the eighteenth century it became a busy port and by the nineteenth century, an industrial area had developed along both sides of the river and along the Forth–Clyde canal (old industrial zones). Next to the industrial zones, tenement housing was built for the workers employed in the factories and docks (old low-cost housing zone). Richer people lived in more expensive housing on the higher ground above the river and away from the noise and smells of the factories (old high-cost housing zone). At the same time, people were moving out of the town centre and housing was being replaced by shops and offices (central business district).

This century, with rail and road transport, people have moved to houses further out of the centre (new high-cost and new low-cost housing) and smaller shopping centres have grown up within the housing areas (new business districts).

Most recently, new industries (new industrial zones) and new shopping centres (new business districts) have been built in the suburbs near main roads.

All these land-use zones are shown on Figure 4.10 and the changes in population density and land values from the centre of Glasgow to the city boundary are shown by **transects** in Figures 4.11 and 4.12.

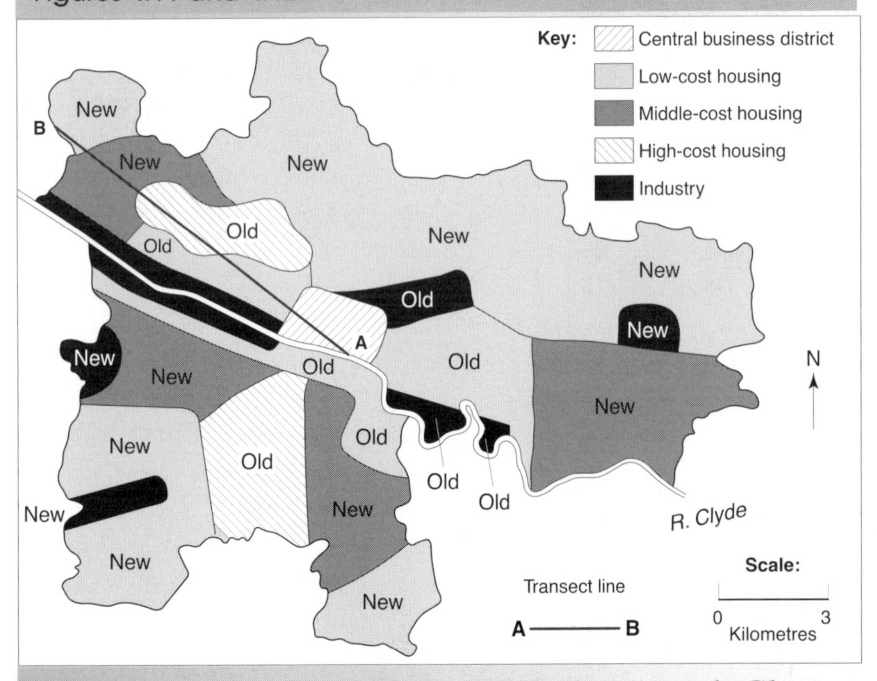

Figure 4.10 Land-use zones in Glasgow.

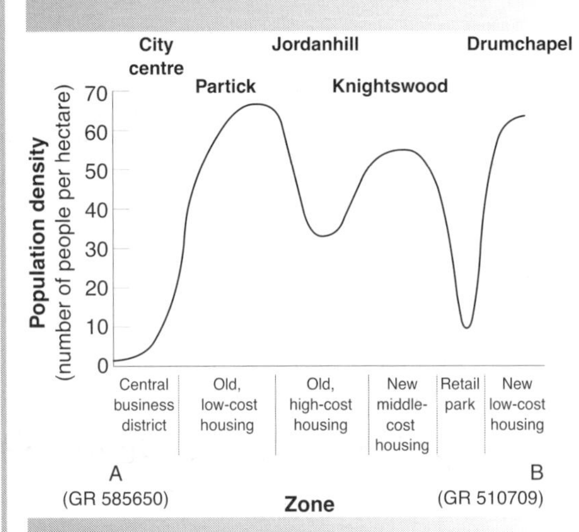

Figure 4.11 Changes in population density from Glasgow city centre to the suburbs (transect line A–B on Figure 4.10).

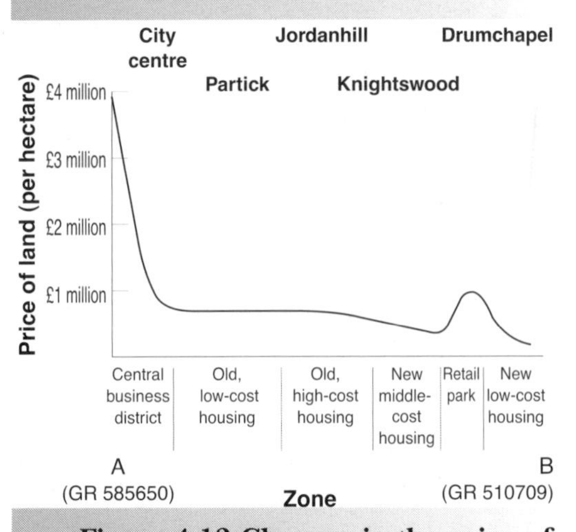

Figure 4.12 Changes in the price of land from Glasgow city centre to the suburbs (transect line A–B on Figure 4.10).

★ RESOURCES ★

Figure 4.13 Tenements in Partick, Glasgow.

Figure 4.14 Jordanhill, Glasgow.

Figure 4.15 New housing in Knightswood, Glasgow.

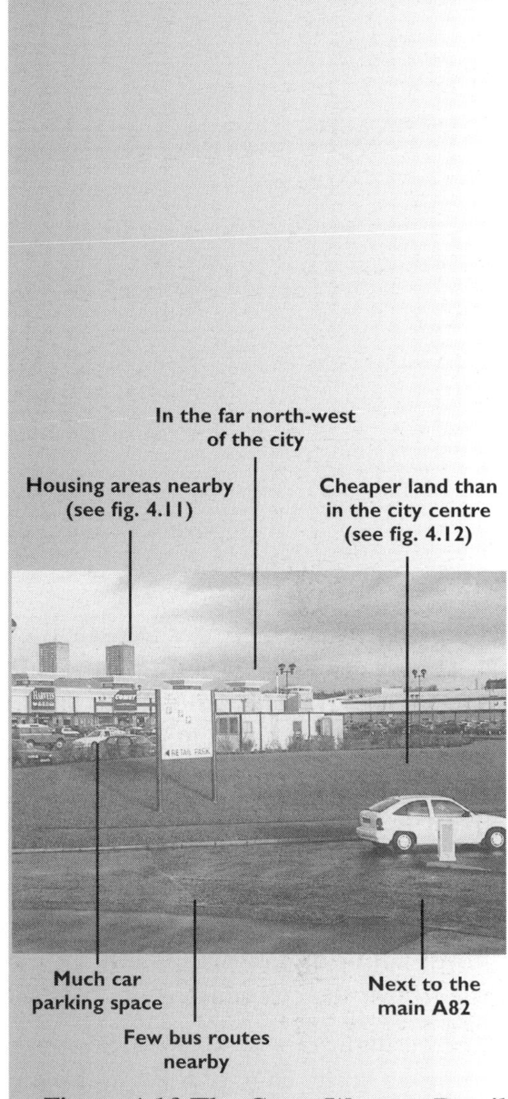

Figure 4.16 The Great Western Retail Park, Glasgow.

Extension Text

4H LAND USE AND LAND VALUES

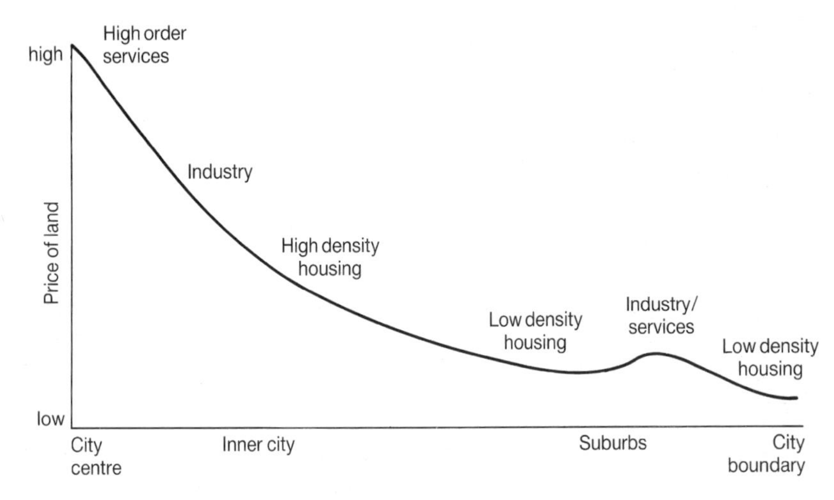

Figure 4.17 Land uses and land values in a city.

The price of land increases towards the centre of a town or city. This is because the city centre is the most accessible location and is in most demand from land users. The only land users that can afford land in the city centre are high-order services. They need a central location to attract the maximum number of customers.

Factory owners can afford to pay quite high prices for land, so factories are found near the CBD or at accessible points in the suburbs (e.g. where main roads meet). Housing is found on the cheapest land in the suburbs. Builders of high-density housing can afford slightly higher prices and high-density housing is found a little nearer the city centre.

Increasingly, new industries, shopping centres and offices are setting up at the edge of town to take advantage of cheap land and lack of congestion.

4J URBAN LAND-USE MODELS

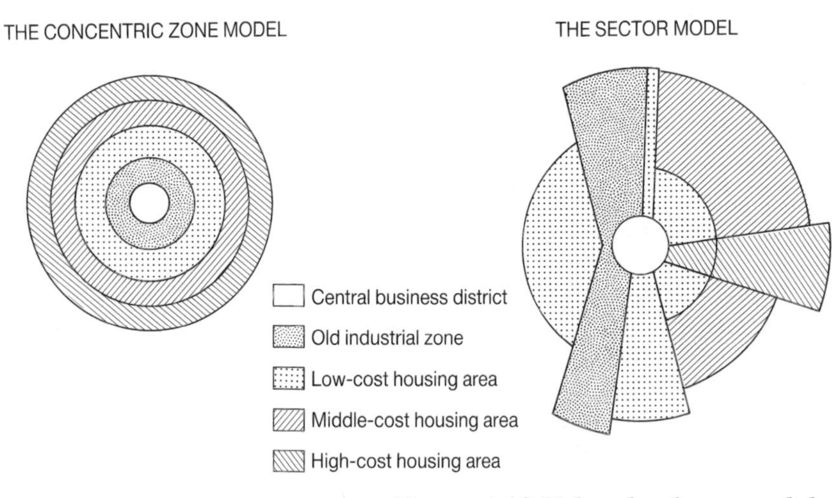

Figure 4.18 Urban land-use models.

If the price of land decreases away from the city centre at the same rate in all directions, the different land uses will form **concentric** circles, as in Figure 4.18. This is the **concentric zone model** of urban land use. However, if some sectors of the city are more attractive than others (for example, if they are near transport routes for industry), then the land uses will form **sectors**, not circles, as in Figure 4.18. This is the **sector model**.

In both these models, the low-cost housing is found in the least attractive location next to the industry, and the high-cost housing is furthest from the industry.

Land use in Hawick	Distance from centre (km)	Cost of land per hectare (£)
Central business district	0	130 000
Old industrial area	0.2	100 000
Low-cost housing area	0.4	90 000
Middle-cost housing area	0.7	80 000
High-cost housing area	1.0	70 000

Figure 4.19 Land values in Hawick.

E Questions

Read the Extension Text.

E1 Why are high-order services found in the CBD?

Look at Figure 4.19.

E2 Explain why the land use changes from the centre to the outskirts of Hawick.

E3 Explain why land-use zones sometimes form sectors.

C Questions

CASE STUDY OF GLASGOW

Look at Figures 4.10 and 4.11.

C1 Compare the changes in land use along the transect line (A–B) through Glasgow with those in the concentric zone model.

Look at Figure 4.12.

C2 Describe the relationship between land use and land value along the transect line (A–B).

Look at Figure 4.11.

C3 Suggest reasons for the changes in population density from the city centre to the suburbs.

C4 Describe the similarities and differences between the housing in Figure 4.13 and Figure 4.15.

Look at Figure 4.16.

C5 Describe the advantages and disadvantages of this location for a retail park.

UNIT 5

Urban Problems and Their Solutions

Core Text

5A URBAN PROBLEMS

As towns grow, they become home to more people who need more houses, more jobs, more services and better transport. At the same time, the older buildings become run-down and need to be replaced. These are some of the most common urban problems which town planners must try to solve. They are shown in Figure 5.1.

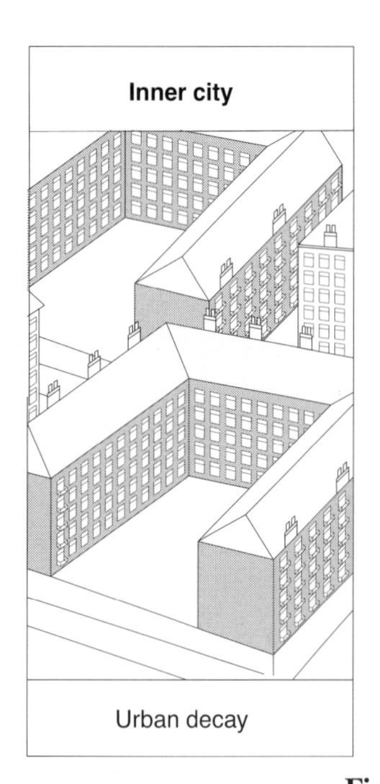

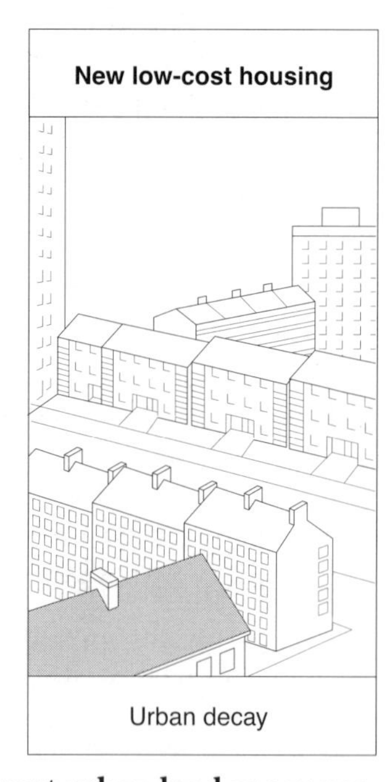

Figure 5.1 The problems of different urban land-use zones.

5B TRAFFIC CONGESTION IN THE CBD

Traffic congestion affects most, if not all, towns and cities in Britain. It happens when too many vehicles are using the roads and the traffic slows down. This can be annoying for people, companies can lose money and it can be dangerous if the emergency services are delayed by congestion. It also causes air and noise pollution and increases the number of accidents.

Causes of traffic congestion	Solutions
• many people owning cars • people driving to the CBD for work, shopping and entertainment • lorries and buses • narrow streets • parking on the street • traffic lights and pedestrian crossings	• ring-roads and by-passes • one-way streets • improved bus and train services • multi-storey car parks • pedestrianised CBDs • 'park and ride' schemes

5C URBAN DECAY IN THE INNER CITY

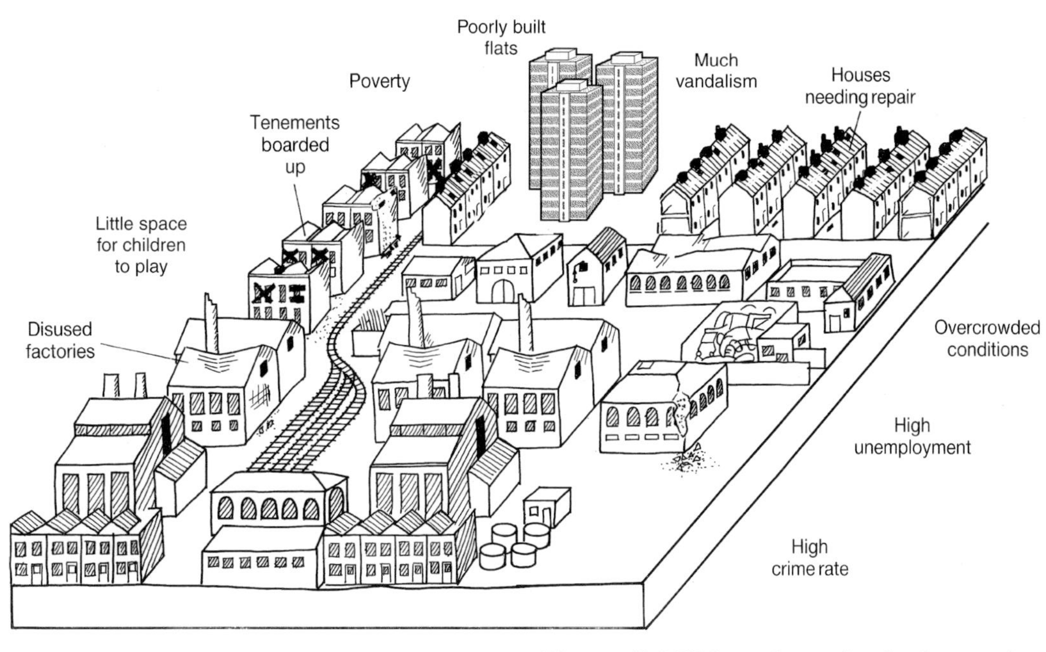

Figure 5.2 Urban decay in the inner city.

Urban decay is the name given to the poor condition of the buildings in towns. Some of these conditions are shown in Figure 5.2. Planners have tried many ways to solve urban decay. In the 1960s, old terraced and tenement housing was pulled down and high-rise tower blocks were built. These new flats had baths, inside toilets and central heating. Unfortunately, they were often poorly built, were unsuitable for young children and old people, and were often vandalised. They now suffer from urban decay themselves.

Planners have also built **New Towns** like East Kilbride, Cumbernauld and Livingston. Here, they could make sure the living conditions were much more pleasant for people. However, New Towns are expensive to build and they did not solve the problems in the inner city, which just became worse.

5D URBAN REGENERATION IN THE INNER CITY

Since the 1980s, urban decay has been tackled by improving many aspects of the inner city, including housing. This is called **urban regeneration** and it involves:

- Renovating (modernising) old housing so people can remain in the same community;
- attracting industries, to reduce unemployment;
- improving the environment by pulling down derelict buildings, planting trees and grass and reducing pollution;
- providing services such as shopping centres, health centres and community centres.

5E URBAN SPRAWL IN THE SUBURBS

As towns get bigger, they grow outwards, swallowing up nearby countryside. This is called **urban sprawl**. It reduces the area of farmland in Britain and it means that people living in the inner city have further to travel to get out of the city.

The causes of urban sprawl are:

- more people want to live in the greener suburbs
- industries want to set up out of town, where it is less congested
- new shopping centres are built at the edge of town on cheaper land
- new by-passes and airports take up more space.

One possible solution to urban sprawl is **Green Belts** – areas around the edges of towns, in which it is very difficult to obtain planning permission to build. They have slowed down urban sprawl but, in some areas, building has simply continued beyond the Green Belt.

Core Questions

Look at Figure 5.1.

1 Name one common problem in most towns in (a) the CBD and (b) the inner city.

Look at 5B.

2 Give two reasons why there is traffic congestion in the centre of towns.

3 In what way does a better train service help to reduce traffic congestion?

Look at 5C.

4 Why were high-rise tower blocks built in the 1960s?

5 Name three New Towns in Scotland.

Look at 5D.

6 Apart from improving the housing, name two ways in which planners now improve the inner city.

7 Choosing from urban sprawl, Green Belt, urban regeneration, urban decay and renovate, which term means:
(a) the poor condition of buildings in a town
(b) to modernise a building
(c) a town growing out into the countryside
(d) the area around a town protected from development
(e) to improve many aspects of the inner city

F Questions

CASE STUDY OF LONDON

Look at Figure 5.6.

F1 Give some of the main reasons for traffic congestion in central London.

Look at Figure 5.7.

F2 Do you think it was a good idea to build the M25? Give reasons for your answer.

Look at Figure 5.8.

F3 Describe some of the problems of living in London's Docklands before 1980.

Look at Figure 5.9.

F4 (a) What are the main changes that have happened in Docklands since 1981?

(b) Do you think these changes have helped the local people? Give reasons for your answer.

Look at Figure 5.10.

F5 As London continues to grow, what is happening to the area around London?

Look at Figure 5.11.

F6 Describe London's Green Belt.

F7 (a) Who wishes to build on the Green Belt?

(b) Do you think they should be allowed to do so? Give reasons for your answer.

G Questions

CASE STUDY OF LONDON

Look at Figure 5.6.

G1 Describe the main causes of traffic congestion in central London.

Look at Figure 5.7.

G2 Which is the better solution to this congestion, (a) the M25 ring road or (b) better rail links into central London? Give reasons for your choice.

Look at Figure 5.8.

G3 Describe the urban decay in London's Docklands before 1980.

Look at Figure 5.9.

G4 Describe one advantage and one disadvantage of the Docklands Development Scheme.

Look at Figure 5.10.

G5 Describe the effects of urban sprawl around London.

Look at Figure 5.11.

G6 Do you agree with the statement that 'London's Green Belt has been a total success.' Give reasons for your answer.

Figure 5.3 Canary Wharf, Docklands, London.

CASE STUDY OF LONDON

Figure 5.4

Introduction

More people live in London than in the whole of Scotland. It has been the biggest settlement in Britain for the last 1,000 years. Due to its size, London's problems are similar to, but bigger than, those of other cities in Britain and it is harder to find solutions.

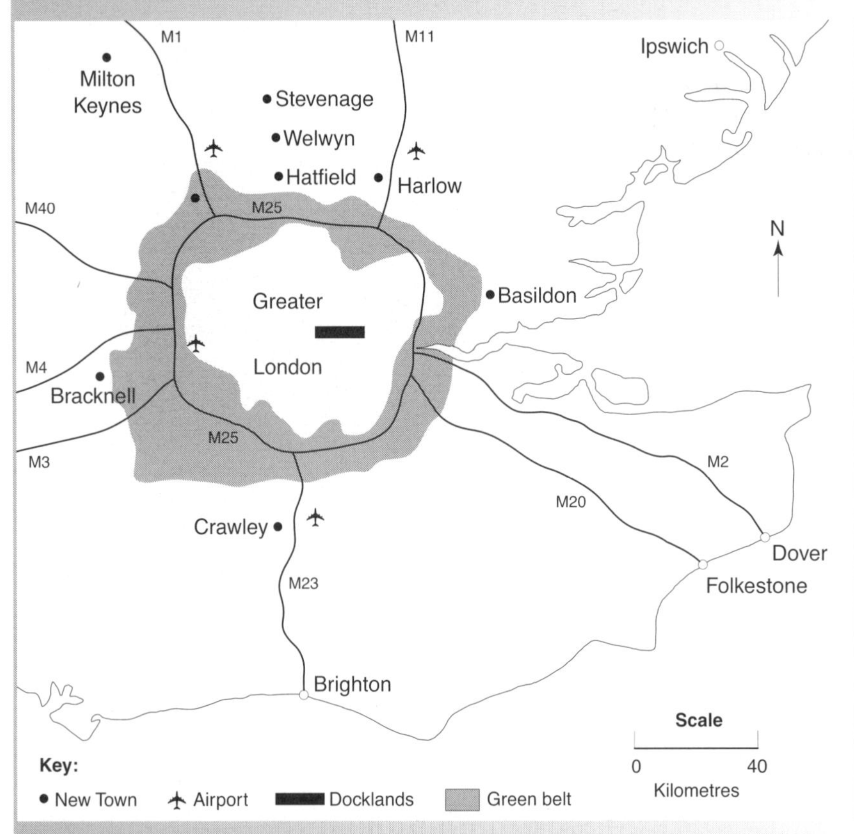

Figure 5.5 The location of London.

Figure 5.6

Traffic Congestion in Central London

The average speed of vehicles in central London in 1908 was 15 km per hour. In 1998, it was still 15 km per hour. Over one million people travel into central London to work each day, and many of them arrive by car during the rush-hour. They are joined by thousands of shoppers and tourists on slow-moving buses and coaches and by delivery lorries, often double-parking while they restock all the shops and offices. These vehicles use roads which are laid out in a grid-iron pattern, so there are many cross-roads, which means many sets of traffic lights. This is why traffic in London moves no faster now than it did 90 years ago.

Figure 5.7

Solutions to Traffic Congestion

One of the best ways of getting people off London's roads has been to build railways – both underground and overground. The first underground railway line was built in 1863. More underground lines are still being built, like the Jubilee Line. Overground, there is now a light railway to Docklands and fast electrified rail links to surrounding towns.

Another solution has been to build the M25 ring-road around London. This was completed in the mid-1980s. Traffic needing to get from one side of London to the other now has no need to go through the centre, causing congestion. The M25 is 190 km long and has up to five lanes in each direction. The M25 occupies a great deal of land that was originally farmland. Land near the motorway is now being taken over by offices, factories and shopping centres, eager to locate beside a motorway. Unfortunately, the M25 is often congested itself, which supports the views of some experts who believe that building new roads only encourages more people to travel by car and does not reduce congestion.

Figure 5.8

Urban Decay in London's Docklands

In the nineteenth century, London's docks were the busiest in the world and provided work for thousands of people and, for every job in the docks, there were three more in the factories and warehouses that lined the docks. The workers lived crowded together in nearby terraced housing.

However, as ships became bigger, the shallow water at the docks became unsuitable and new ports were built downstream. By 1981, all London's docks had closed and male unemployment was 30 per cent. At the same time, the old terraced housing was in need of improvement. Many houses lacked facilities and some had suffered bomb damage during the Second World War (1939–45). Many houses were pulled down in the 1950s and '60s and high-rise blocks were built. But these were failures and only added to the urban decay (see Figure 5.12).

In 1981, the London Docklands Development Corporation was set up to regenerate the area. Its results are shown in Figure 5.9.

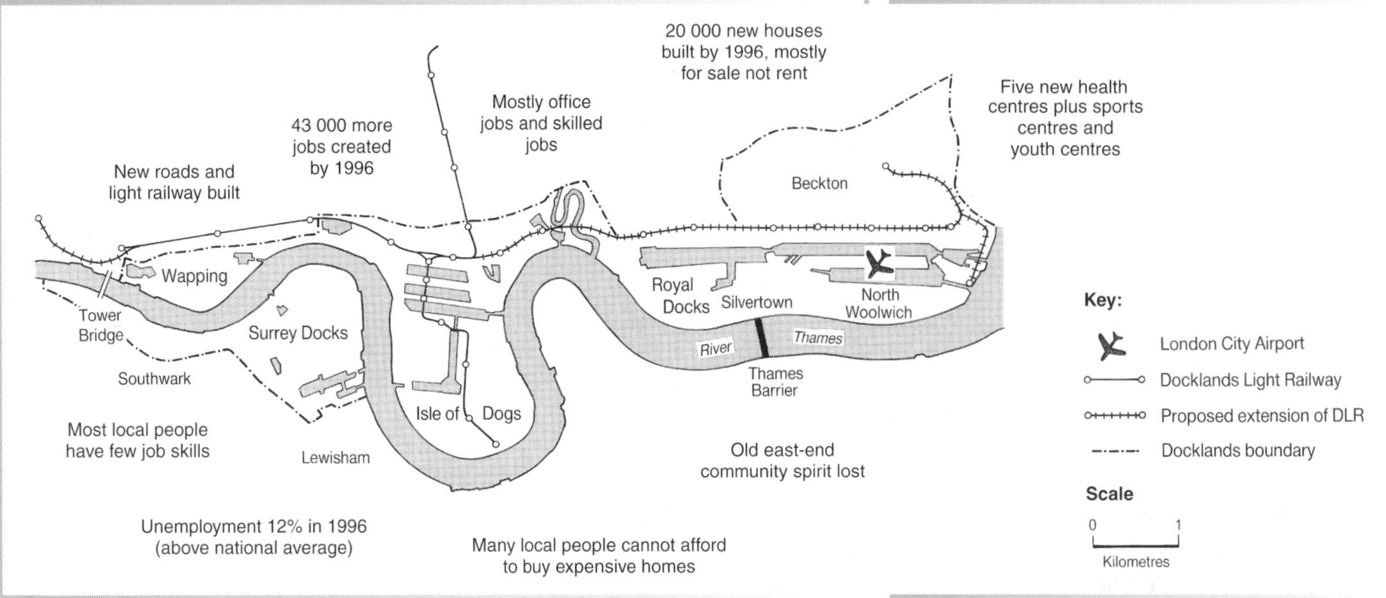

Figure 5.9 The Docklands Development Scheme.

Figure 5.10

Urban Sprawl Around London

London now covers an area 30 times larger than it did in 1800. As it has spread into the countryside, valuable farmland has been lost and whole villages, such as Wimbledon and Hampstead, have been swallowed up. This happened firstly because of the railways and, more recently, because of cars and better roads, which allow people to **commute** long distances into the centre of London to work. But, as people with higher incomes move out to the suburbs and beyond, inner London is left to the old, the poor and the **immigrant** communities who cannot afford to live elsewhere.

Figure 5.11

London's Green Belt

The Green Belt is a 25 km wide zone of land around London, within which it is very difficult to obtain permission to build (see Figure 5.5). It was set up in 1938 to stop London expanding further. Sixty years later, over 90 per cent of the Green Belt is still countryside, but there is increasing pressure to build on it. The M25 was built mostly on Green Belt land, which has made the area around the motorway very attractive for housing, shopping centres, offices and factories. Although the Green Belt has stopped urban sprawl at the edge of London, building has occurred beyond the Green Belt, taking over countryside even further from London.

Figure 5.12 High-rise problems.

Extension Text

5F URBAN DECAY AND URBAN RENEWAL

The problems faced by areas of urban decay fall into three categories:

1 **environmental problems** such as sub-standard housing, poorly built flats, waste land, pollution and overcrowding.
2 **economic problems** such as declining industries, high unemployment, low standards of living, lack of space for new industry and lack of skilled workers.
3 **social problems** such as high crime rate and a high percentage of disadvantaged people (such as the elderly, immigrants and single parents).

Urban renewal is the name given to the various ways in which planners have tackled the problems of urban decay. There have been two main approaches:

1 **Urban redevelopment** – the wholesale clearance of buildings, common in the 1960s. It led to a large **overspill population** of people who were forced to move out of the inner cities.
2 **Urban regeneration** – the improvement of housing, industry, services and the environment, common in the 1980s and 1990s. Renovation was more common than the clearance of buildings. The government has encouraged this by setting up Urban Development Corporations (UDCs) in England and Wales, such as London Docklands and Merseyside Docklands.

5G URBAN POPULATION CHANGE

Urban decay and renewal in the last 40 years have led to a redistribution of the population within and around cities. These changes are summarised in the table below.

	CBD	Inner city	Suburbs	Urban–rural fringe	Remote countryside
Population change	decreasing	decreasing	increasing	increasing	decreasing
Reasons	noise and air pollution; high land prices	crime; air pollution; urban decay	new private housing schemes; near new industrial estates	within commuting distance of city; quieter; cheaper land	lack of jobs; lack of services
Population structure	many people in poorer sections of community (for example, elderly people, immigrants, students, young people)		high percentage of people with higher incomes (for example, middle-aged people, people with professional and managerial careers)		elderly people; people with few qualifications

Figure 5.13 Population change in urban and rural areas.

E Questions

Read the Extension Text.

E1 What is meant by (a) urban renewal, and (b) overspill population?

E2 Explain the meaning of the following statement: 'Urban redevelopment took the heart out of British cities.'

E3 Why is the term urban regeneration used to describe urban renewal in the 1980s?

E4 Which areas within cities are (a) increasing in population and (b) decreasing in population?

C Questions

CASE STUDY OF LONDON

Look at Figures 5.8 and 5.9.

C1 Describe the different points of view people might have towards the Docklands Development Scheme.

Look at Figures 5.7 and 5.10.

C2 Describe the main causes of urban sprawl around London.

Look at Figure 5.11.

C3 Do you think London's Green Belt will exist in 20 years time? Give reasons for your answer.

Look at Figures 5.6 and 5.7.

C4 Describe the arguments for and against widening the M25.

C5 Do you agree with the statement that 'With more commuters and more tourists, London's traffic problem is only going to get worse'. Give reasons for your answer.

UNIT 6

Skills in Industrial Studies

Core Text

6A INTRODUCTION TO INDUSTRIAL STUDIES

Some of the most obvious parts of any town are its factories, and some of the most striking parts of the countryside are its quarries and mines. They might not be the most attractive sights, but they are important parts of the landscape and one of our tasks in Geography is to find out where they are found and why they are there.

For the Standard Grade examination, you need to know and understand the following:

1 the different types and sectors of industry
2 the reasons why industry sets up in particular locations
3 how the Government affects industry
4 why the location of industries changes over time
5 the effects on the local area of an industrial site opening or closing.

You also need to develop the following enquiry skills:

1 how to gather information on industry – by observing and recording, and by fieldsketching
2 how to process this information – by drawing pie-graphs and by labelling (**annotating**) fieldsketches.

6B GATHERING INFORMATION

There are several ways of gathering information about industry. For example, to find out about the topics studied in units 7–10, some of the following gathering techniques might be used:

Figure 6.1

Topic studied	Gathering technique
Sectors of industry	**extracting information** from the Census, Yellow Pages and trade directories
Location of industry	**interviewing** company representatives

Figure 6.1 continued

Topic studied	Gathering technique
Industrial landscapes	**fieldsketching** **observing and recording** traffic, building types, land uses, environmental quality
Changing industry	**observing and recording** present-day industries **extracting information** from old maps on past industries
Effects of industries opening/closing	**compiling and using a questionnaire** **interviewing** people affected

6C OBSERVING AND RECORDING ENVIRONMENTAL QUALITY

Environmental quality is the attractiveness and cleanliness of an area. You can gather information on environmental quality by making up an **environmental quality index**.

- List the aspects of the area you are surveying, for example, the state of the buildings, the amount of greenery, the amount of traffic, the litter, the graffiti, the air pollution (Figure 6.2).
- Each aspect should be given a mark out of 10, according to how clean/attractive it is, for example, if there is no graffiti, award 10 marks.
- As a guide to help you decide how many marks to award, write descriptions of the worst and best quality you might expect (see Figure 6.2).
- Survey your area, giving a mark out of 10 for each aspect.
- Add up the marks and the total gives you the environmental quality index for that area. For example, in Table 6.2 Kingsway Science Park scored 49 out of a possible 60.
- This index can then be compared with those for other areas. For example, in Figure 6.3, Kingsway has a much higher environmental quality than Canal Way industrial area.

Figure 6.2

ENVIRONMENTAL QUALITY INDEX

Poor quality (0)	←Points→	High quality (10)
ugly, badly-maintained buildings		clean, attractive buildings
bad air pollution		no air pollution
a lot of graffiti and vandalism		no graffiti or vandalism
no greenery visible a lot of derelict land		lots of trees and grass no derelict land
a lot of litter		no litter

Figure 6.3

ENVIRONMENTAL QUALITY INDEX	Kingsway Science Park	Canal Way industrial area
buildings	5	2
air pollution	7	3
graffiti/vandalism	8	1
greenery	9	5
derelict land	10	4
litter	10	2
TOTAL	49	17

6D FIELDSKETCHING AN INDUSTRIAL AREA

- Take sheets of plain paper, a clipboard, pencil and rubber.
- Find a suitable site where you can see the whole of the area clearly.
- On your paper, make a frame for your sketch.
- Draw the outline shape of the buildings.
- Put in all their relevant characteristics, such as chimneys, windows and the number of storeys.
- Draw in the roads and any other lines of communication.
- Include any other relevant features, such as waste tips, greenery and nearby housing.
- Around the frame, label the main features of the sketch.
- Give the sketch a title and include its location (usually a grid reference) and the direction in which you were facing.

6E DRAWING A PIE-GRAPH

A pie-graph is used to show how one total is divided up.

- Pie-graphs are circles divided into slices or segments.
- Each segment shows an amount – the bigger the segment, the bigger the amount.
- Each segment is worked out in degrees – the segments together add up to 360°.
- To draw a pie-graph, work out the number of degrees in each of your segments (see 6F).
- Draw a circle, then draw the first segment in pencil, starting from the top of the circle and going clockwise.
- You may find it easier to start with the smallest segment.
- Use a protractor to measure the size of each segment.
- Draw the second smallest segment next to the first.
- Work out where it ends, either by using a protractor or by adding on its degrees to the total so far.
- Complete all the segments.
- Shade in and label each segment.
- Give the pie-graph a title.

Figure 6.4

Types of industry in Kingsway Science Park

Type of industry	Number of companies	Number of degrees (to the nearest whole number)
electronics	20	144°
research organisations	4	29°
software engineering	11	79°
medical instruments	5	36°
drugs manufacture	10	72°
TOTAL	50	360°

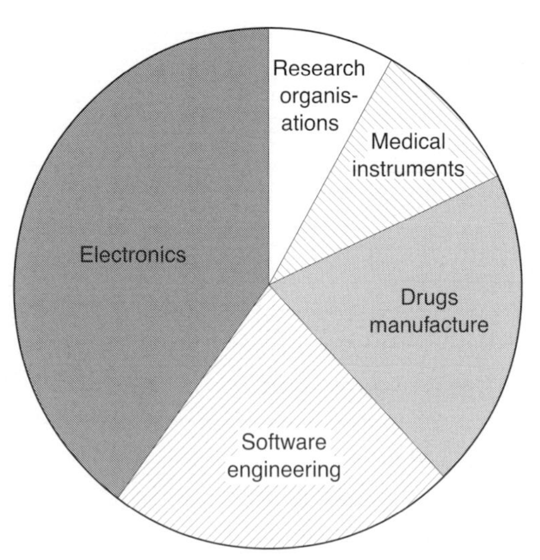

Figure 6.5 Types of industry at Kingsway Science Park.

6F CALCULATING THE DEGREES FOR A PIE-GRAPH

To calculate the number of degrees for each segment of a pie-graph:

- Add up the total number to be represented by all the segments (50 companies in Figure 6.4).
- For each segment, divide its number by the total and then multiply by 360 – this gives you the number of degrees for that segment (in Figure 6.4, electronics = $20 \div 50 \times 360 = 144°$.
- Repeat this calculation for all the segments.
- Check that the total number of degrees adds up 360.

6G ANNOTATING A FIELDSKETCH

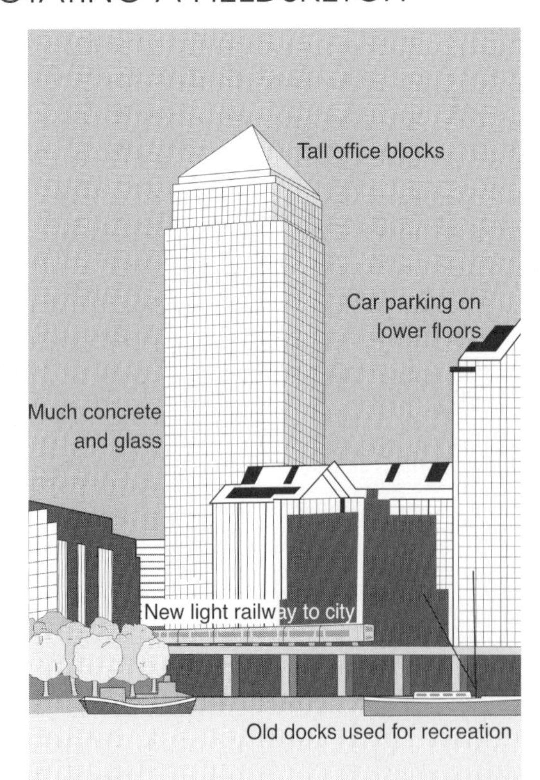

Figure 6.6 An annotated fieldsketch of Canary Wharf as shown in Figure 5.3.

To annotate a fieldsketch:

- Make a neat copy of your fieldsketch.
- Only label the features that are important to your study, for example, if you are comparing an old and a new industrial area, you might label types of transport, chimneys, number of storeys and building materials.
- Write each label clearly beside the feature, using arrows if necessary but making sure they do not cross.
- Do not write too much information on your sketch, otherwise it will become too cluttered.

F Questions

Look at 6B.

F1 Which technique would you use (a) to find out the reasons why a company set up in your local area and (b) to look at changes in an industrial area in the last 10 years?

Look at 6C.

F2 If you wanted to find out the environmental quality of an industrial area, name two aspects of the environment you would study.

Look at 6D.

F3 (a) Draw a fieldsketch of the area shown in Figure 6.7.
(b) Label the sketch to show the main land uses in the area.

Figure 6.7 Aerial view of a new industrial area.

Look at 6E.

F4 (a) Copy the pie-graph in Figure 6.8.
(b) Complete the pie-graph, using the information in Figure 6.9.

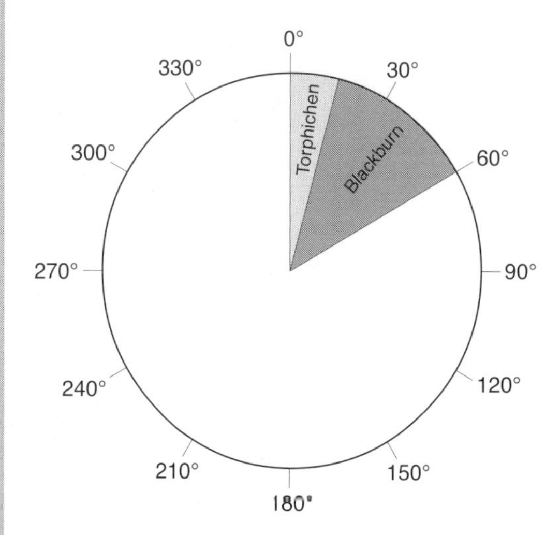

Figure 6.8 Homes of workers in a Bathgate factory.

Figure 6.9

Homes of workers at a Bathgate factory

Town/village	Number of workers	Number of degrees
Bathgate	30	150°
Armadale	18	90°
Blackburn	9	45°
Whitburn	12	60°
Torphichen	3	15°
TOTAL	72	

Look at Figures 6.10 and 6.11.

F5 Which table of information – Figure 6.10 or 6.11 – would be better shown on a pie-graph?

Figure 6.10

Sector of industry	Percentage of workers in Scotland
Primary	5%
Secondary	32%
Tertiary	63%

Figure 6.11

Year	Number of workers in Bentley Shoe Company
1961	3800
1971	3900
1981	4200
1991	3300

Figure 6.12

Features of factory buildings	Percentage of factories with this feature
chimneys	40%
lorry parks	15%
landscaping	25%
brick walls	50%
2 or more storeys	35%

G Questions

Look at 6B.

G1 Which technique would you use (a) to compare the types of industry in two industrial areas and (b) to investigate the effects of a factory closing down? Give a reason for each answer.

Look at 6C.

G2 If you were investigating the environmental quality of an old industrial area, which aspects of the environment would you study?

Look at 6D.

G7 (a) Draw a fieldsketch of the light industrial area shown in Figure 6.7.
(b) Annotate the fieldsketch to show its main characteristics.

Figure 6.13

Local people's views on new cement works	% of people	Number of degrees
very much in favour	32	115
in favour	15	54
no opinion	6	22
against	19	68
very much against	28	101
TOTAL	100	

Look at 6E.

G4 Draw a pie-graph to show the information on views about a new cement works in Figure 6.13.

Look at Figures 6.10 and 6.11.

G5 Which table of information – Figure 6.10 or 6.11 – would be best shown on a pie-graph? Give a reason for your answer.

C Questions

Look at 6B.

C1 Which technique would you use (a) to compare the landscape of two industrial areas and (b) to investigate changes in an industrial area over the last 20 years? Justify your choice of techniques.

Look at 6C.

C2 Describe how you would gather information on the environmental quality of an industrial area.

Look at 6D.

C3 (a) Draw a fieldsketch of the industrial area shown in Figure 6.7.
(b) Annotate the sketch to show the evidence that it is a new industrial area.

Look at 6E and 6F.

C4 Draw a pie-graph of the information in the table below.

Sector of industry	Number of workers in one small town
Primary	300
Secondary	3300
Tertiary	5400

Look at Figures 6.10, 6.11 and 6.12.

C5 Which table of information – Figure 6.10, 6.11 or 6.12 – would be best shown on a pie-graph? Give a reason for your answer.

UNIT 7

Sectors of Industry

Core Text

7A SECTORS OF INDUSTRY

The work people do for a living is called **industry**. There are three sectors of industry.

1 **Primary industry** is based on working with the resources of the land or sea, for example, farming, mining and fishing.
2 **Manufacturing industry** is based on making products, for example, shipbuilding, making furniture and building houses.
3 **Service industry** is based on providing a service to others, for example, nursing, teaching and working in a bank.

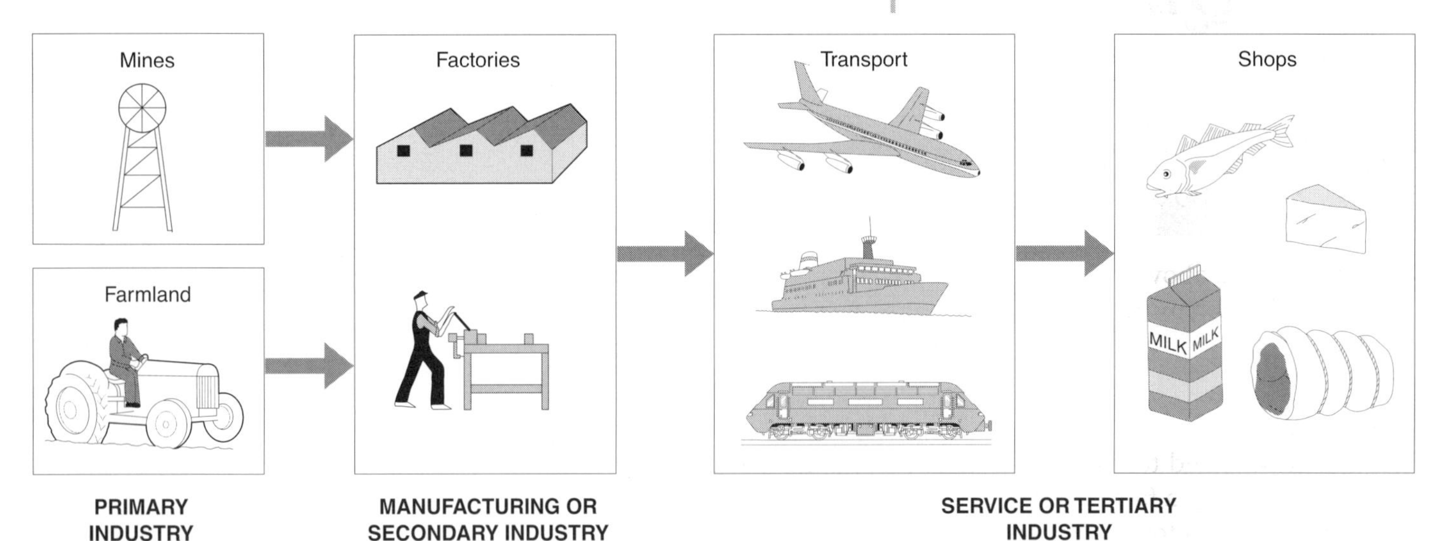

Figure 7.1 The industrial system.

Manufacturing industries make the goods we need. To make goods, they need the **raw materials** produced by primary industry. Once the goods have been made, they need people in the service industry to transport them and sell them.

7B LOCATION OF MANUFACTURING INDUSTRY

Primary industries are found at the source of the raw materials, for example, where there are minerals to be mined, fish to be caught or land to be farmed. Most service industries are found in towns

Figure 7.2 Factors affecting the location of manufacturing industry.

and cities where many people live. But deciding on a location for a manufacturing industry is more difficult. Many important facts, called **factors**, must be taken into account. These are shown in Figure 7.2.

Core Questions

Look at 7A.

doctor	car worker	oil rig worker	professional footballer
coal miner	forestry worker	accountant	
train-driver	baker	engineer	

1 Which of the above jobs are in (a) primary, (b) manufacturing and (c) service industries?
2 What do you think are the main raw materials needed to make (a) cars and (b) garden sheds?

Look at 7B.

4 Companies need to consider seven factors before deciding where to set up a factory. One factor is a suitable site. What are the other six factors?

Figure 7.3

Whisky distilleries are located near a skilled workforce.
Dairies are located close to the shops where their goods are sold.
Paper mills are located near forests.
Aluminium works are located close to a source of cheap electricity.
Electronics factories are located in places where they can obtain grants from the government.
Car works are located where there are good communications.

5 Which of the industries listed in Figure 7.3 is located:
(a) near its power supply
(b) near its market
(c) near the source of its raw materials
(d) near good transport facilities
(e) near a labour force
(f) where there is government aid?

6 What type of site would be needed for a large factory?

F Questions

CASE STUDY OF SCOTLAND

Look at Figure 7.6.

F1 Which sector of industry is most important in all three regions of Scotland?

F2 Which region has the most workers in (a) primary, (b) manufacturing and (c) service industries?

Look at Figure 7.5.

F3 Name two important service industries in (a) the Highlands and (b) the Southern Uplands.

F4 Where is most manufacturing industry in Scotland found?

Look at Figures 7.7, 7.8 and 7.9.

F5 Give two advantages of setting up factories in (a) the Central Lowlands, (b) the Southern Uplands and (c) the Highlands.

F6 Describe two problems in setting up factories in (a) the Southern Uplands and (b) the Highlands.

G Questions

CASE STUDY OF SCOTLAND

Look at Figure 7.6.

G1 Compare the importance of primary industries in the Highlands, Central Lowlands and Southern Uplands.

G2 Compare the importance of service industries in the Highlands, Central Lowlands and Southern Uplands.

Look at Figure 7.5.

G3 Describe the distribution of manufacturing industry in Scotland.

Look at Figure 7.7.

G4 Describe the advantages of the Central Lowlands for manufacturing industry.

Look at Figures 7.8 and 7.9.

G5 Describe two problems shared by the Highlands and the Southern Uplands in attracting industry.

G6 Would you expect more manufacturing industry on the east or west coast of the Highlands? Give reasons for your answer.

CASE STUDY OF SCOTLAND

Figure 7.4

Introduction

Until 1800, most people in Scotland worked in primary industry, especially in farming. By 1900, most people worked in manufacturing industry, especially steelmaking, engineering and shipbuilding. Today, over half of the people in Scotland work in service industries.

Figure 7.5 shows that industries in Scotland, especially manufacturing industries, are not evenly spread. Each region has some advantages and some disadvantages for manufacturing industry. These are shown in Figures 7.7, 7.8 and 7.9.

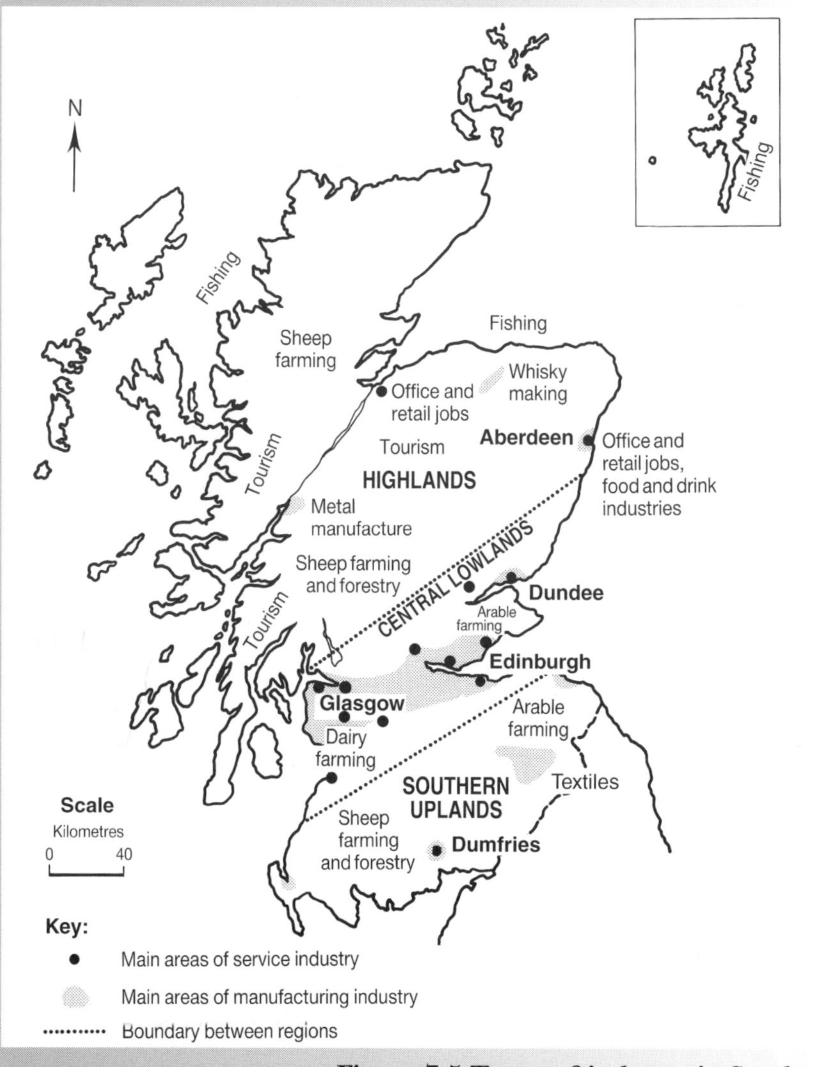

Figure 7.5 Types of industry in Scotland.

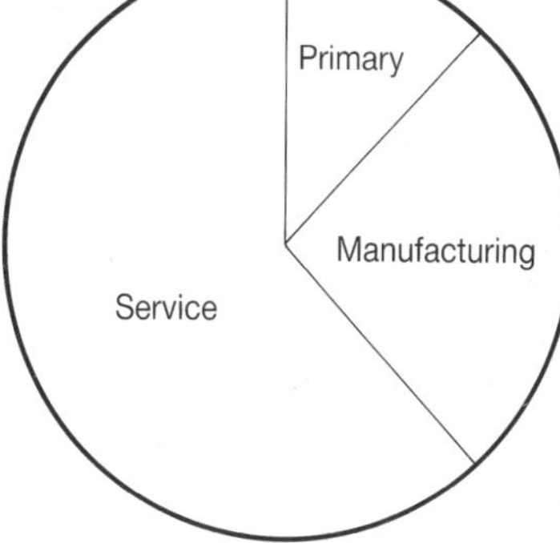

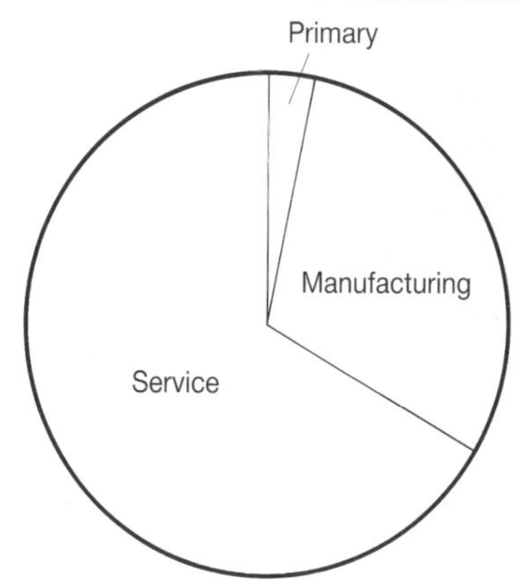

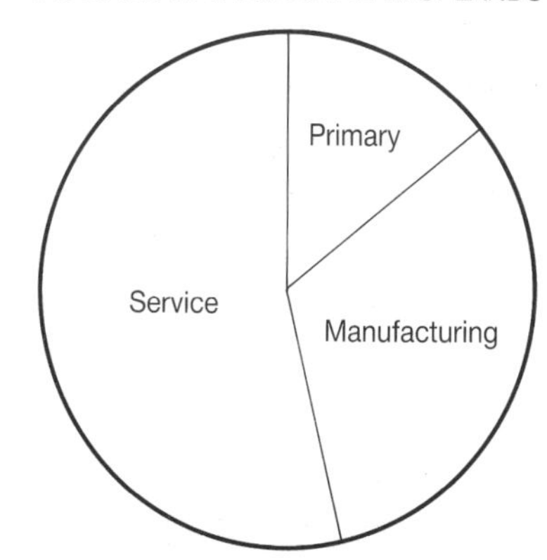

Figure 7.6 Sectors of industry in Scotland.

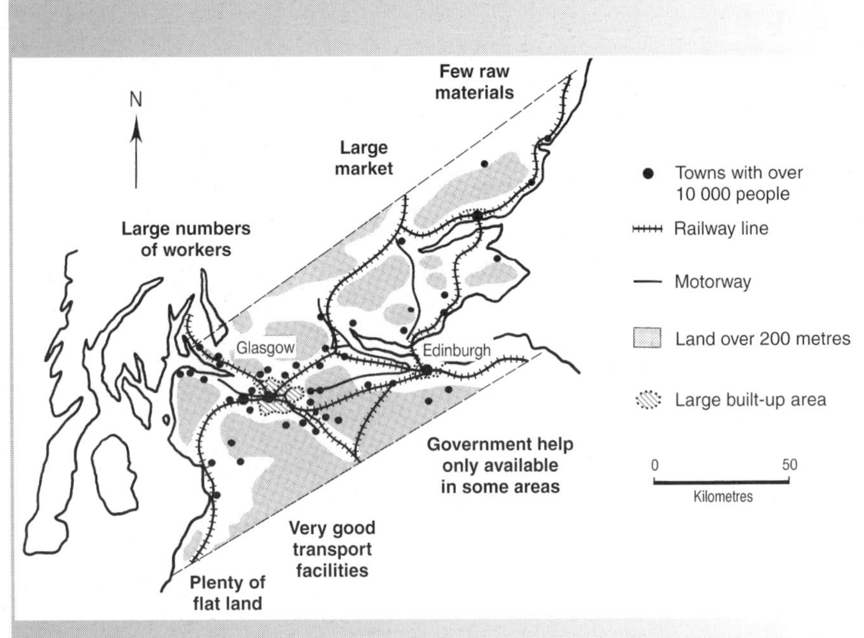

Figure 7.7 The Central Lowlands: suitability for industry.

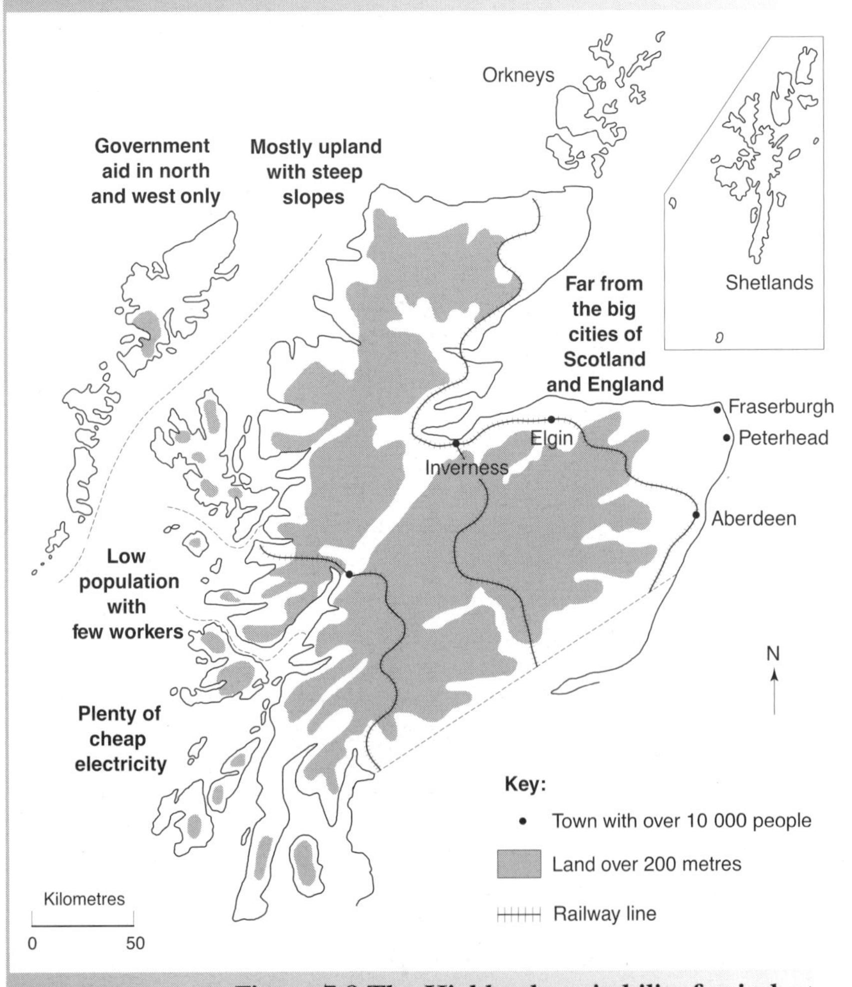

Figure 7.8 The Highlands: suitability for industry.

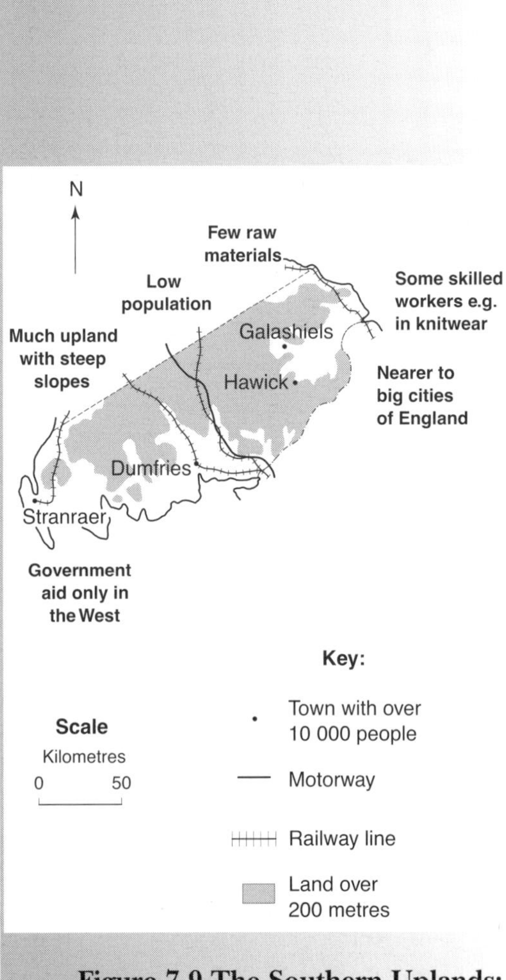

Figure 7.9 The Southern Uplands: suitability for industry.

Extension Text

7C FACTORS AFFECTING THE LOCATION OF INDUSTRY

Nearness to market

A factory's market is where its products are sold. They may be **consumer goods** sold to the public (for example, CDs or watches), or they may be **capital goods**, sold to other factories (for example, machines). Being near to its market reduces a factory's transport costs. If its finished product is heavy, fragile or perishable, it is especially important for the factory to locate near its market.

Nearness to raw materials

A factory's raw materials may come from a primary industry (for example, a furniture factory requires timber), or they may come from another secondary industry (for example, a car factory requires sheet steel). Being near to a source of raw materials reduces transport costs. The heavier the raw materials, the more important it is to locate close to their source.

Transport facilities

The better the transport facilities, the quicker and cheaper it is for factories to bring in raw materials and send out finished goods. Different secondary industries use different transport facilities, as is shown in Figure 7.10.

Figure 7.10

Type of transport	Speed	Cost	Goods carried
air	very quick	expensive	high-value, low-weight goods (for example, cashmere jumpers)
water	very slow	cheap	low-value, high-weight goods (for example, bananas)
road	quick over short distances	quite expensive	small loads (for example, books)
rail	quick over long distances	quite expensive	large loads (for example, coal)

Power supply

All factories use machines, which need power to operate. If the power supply is electricity, this does not affect industrial location much because it is available all over the country at a similar price. In the nineteenth century, the main source of power was coal. Being very bulky and expensive to move, factories were often located on or near coalfields.

Labour supply

If an industry uses a large workforce, it needs to locate near a large town. If a factory requires skilled workers, it will be located where people have the necessary skills.

Regional aid

The government and the European Union offer incentives such as grants and loans to encourage factories to locate in certain areas, such as areas of high unemployment. If there is a choice of several locations for a factory, this factor may be critical in deciding the best location.

Site

Once the best area for locating a manufacturing industry has been decided, the exact site must be chosen. Flat, dry, stable land is necessary, with space nearby for future expansion.

E Questions

Look at Figure 7.1.

E1 What is meant by secondary and tertiary industries?

Read the Extension Text.

E2 Which types of industry need to be near (a) their raw materials and (b) their market?

E3 Explain why different transport facilities would be used to send quantities of diamonds and gravel over long distances.

C Questions

CASE STUDY OF SCOTLAND

Look at Figure 7.6.

C1 **Employment structure** is the proportion of people employed in the three sectors of industry. Compare the employment structure of the Highlands, Central Lowlands and Southern Uplands.

Look at Figure 7.7.

C2 Describe the advantages and disadvantages of the Central Lowlands as a location for manufacturing industry.

Look at Figures 7.8 and 7.9.

C3 Compare the suitability of the Highlands and Southern Uplands for manufacturing industry.

C4 Suggest reasons for the distribution of manufacturing industry in the Southern Uplands, shown in Figure 7.5.

C5 Explain the likely distribution of manufacturing industry in the Highlands.

UNIT 8

Heavy Industry

Core Text

8A HEAVY INDUSTRY

A **heavy industry** is a manufacturing industry that uses heavy or bulky raw materials to make heavy or bulky goods, such as bricks or cement.

8B LOCATION OF HEAVY INDUSTRIES

Heavy industries set up in locations where they are:

1. **near raw materials** – because their raw materials are so heavy, it costs too much to carry them long distances, so cement works are found near limestone, brickworks near clay and engineering works near steel
2. **near a power supply** – many heavy industries began in the nineteenth century, when coal was the main source of power and, because coal is so bulky, most factories set up on or near coalfields
3. **near cheap transport** – because the raw materials are heavy, cheap transport is needed and railways are often used as, in the past, were canals
4. **on flat land** – heavy industries are often very large and need a large area of flat land to build on.

8C IRON AND STEEL MAKING

Figure 8.1 shows how the best location for the iron and steel industry has changed over the last 200 years.

Location 1

Before 1800, the best location was (a) near the raw materials – iron ore and limestone, (b) near a power supply – wood (made into charcoal) to smelt the iron, and (c) near running water to drive the machines. The industry was located in forests, beside running water, where iron ore and limestone were found.

Location 2

After 1800, coal (made into coke) replaced wood as the fuel to heat the iron and drive the machines. There was cheap transport now in the form of canals and railways. So, the industry

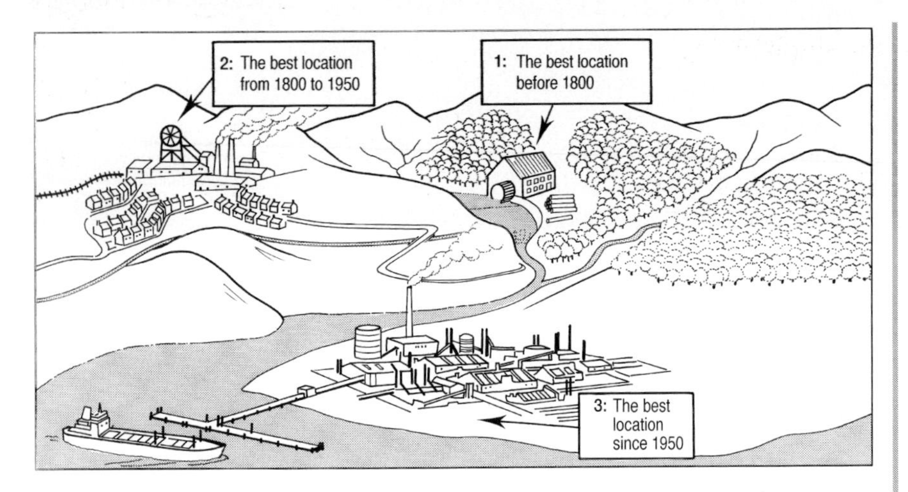

Figure 8.1 The changing locations of the iron and steel industry.

was sited on or near coalfields, and located beside canals and railways.

Location 3

After 1950, iron ore had to be imported from abroad, and steelworks had become very large, so they sited on very large areas of flat land located near coastal ports.

8D THE SHIPBUILDING INDUSTRY

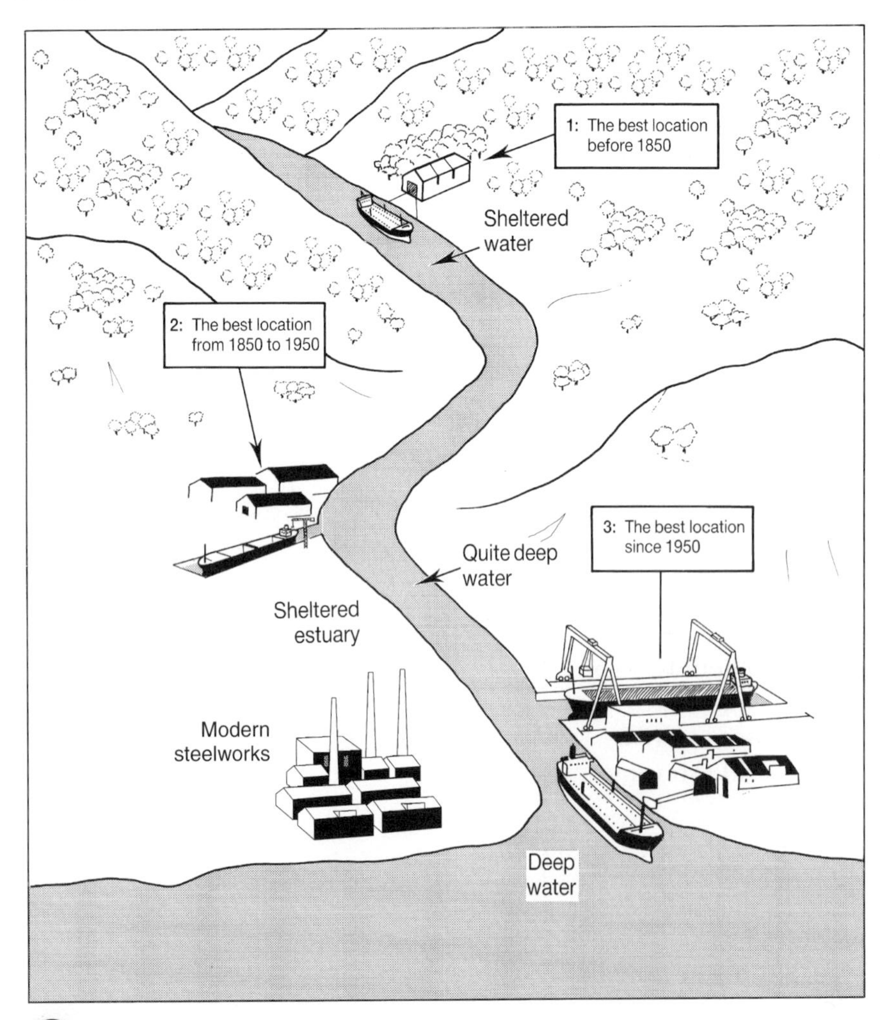

Figure 8.2 The changing locations of the shipbuilding industry.

Figure 8.2 shows how the best location for the shipbuilding industry has changed over the last 200 years.

Location 1

Before 1850, the raw material of the shipbuilding industry was mainly wood, and the industry was situated near forests and sheltered water.

Location 2

Between 1850 and 1950, ships were made from metal and the raw material used was steel. As ships were now bigger, a site was required that was near quite deep, sheltered water.

Location 3

After 1950, ships and shipbuilding works became bigger and a location was needed that was a large area of flat land, beside very deep water.

8E HEAVY INDUSTRY IN SCOTLAND

In the 1800s, central Scotland became one of the world's most important industrial areas. The four main industries at that time were coal-mining, iron- and steelmaking, shipbuilding and engineering.

The iron and steel industry was located on Clydeside, where coal and iron ore were mined. The shipyards were also found along the Clyde where there was nearby steel and deep water. By the turn of the twentieth century, one-fifth of all the ships in the world were launched on the Clyde. There were 560 coal-mines and over 100 blast furnaces making iron in central Scotland, together with a vast range of other heavy industries, making railway lines, steel bridges, boilers and machinery.

This success did not last. After the 1920s, Scotland's heavy industries began to decline. Now, only one coal-mine remains open in Scotland. The last big steelworks at Ravenscraig, near Motherwell, closed in 1992. With no coal nearby, its location was too far from its raw materials, some of which came from as far away as Canada and Russia. Only a few Scottish shipyards remain open and their future is uncertain, partly because there is no longer any steel made nearby and the Firth of Clyde is not deep enough for the largest ships.

8F ELECTRICITY POWER STATIONS

Electricity is made or **generated** in power stations. There are many types of power station, and they use different forms of energy as raw materials.

Coal-fired power stations are built:
- near coal supplies
- on large areas of flat land
- beside water for cooling.

Oil-fired power stations are built:
- on large areas of flat land
- beside deep water, to allow oil tankers to dock.

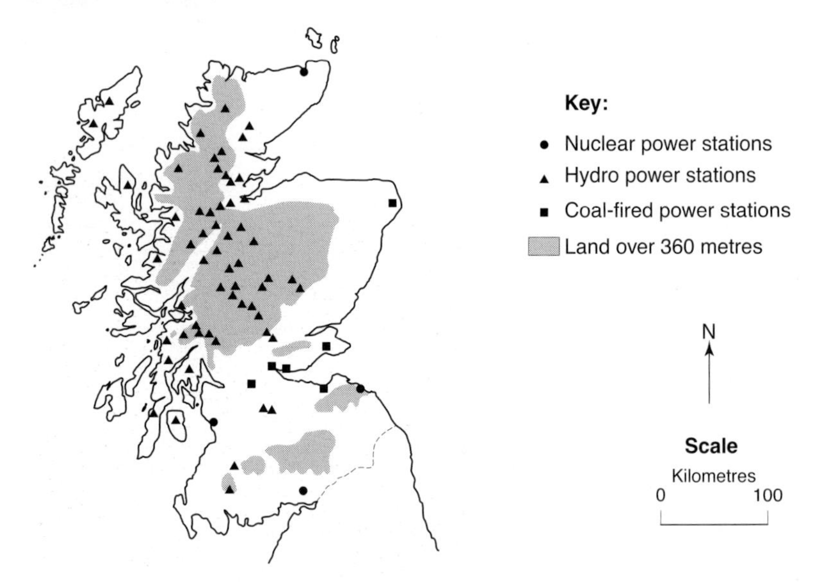

Figure 8.3 Power stations in Scotland.

Hydro-electric power stations are built:

- in areas of high rainfall
- where there are fast-flowing streams
- in uplands where dams can be built across valleys to provide a supply of water.

Nuclear power stations are built:

- on large areas of flat land
- far from towns and cities in case of accidents
- on coasts, because they use vast amounts of water.

Core Questions

Look at 8A.

1 Which of the following industries are heavy industries: making jeans, making steel, making oil-rigs, making cameras, making railway engines?

Look at 8B.

2 Why do heavy industries need to be near their raw materials?

Look at 8C.

3 Why did iron works first set up in forests?

4 Why do modern steelworks set up on coasts?

Look at 8D.

5 Why do shipyards today need to be beside very deep water?

Look at 8E.

6 Why did iron- and steelworks set up on Clydeside in the 1800s?

7 Why did Clydeside become important for shipbuilding in the 1800s?

8 How important was central Scotland for heavy industry at the turn of the twentieth century?

Look at 8F.

9 Which type of power station sets up:

(a) beside deep water

(b) far from cities
(c) beside fast-flowing water
(d) on coalfields?

F Questions

CASE STUDY OF NORTH-EAST ENGLAND

Look at Figure 8.5.

F1 What have been the main heavy industries in north-east England?
F2 When did they become important?

Look at Figure 8.8.

F3 Where were most of these heavy industries found?

Look at Figure 8.7.

F4 What were the main reasons why steelmaking began here in the 1800s?
F5 What were the main reasons why these began to close?
F6 Do you think Teesside is still a suitable place for making steel? Give reasons for your answer.

Look at Figure 8.10.

F7 What were the main reasons why shipbuilding became important?

Look at Figure 8.11.

F8 (a) What type of power station is most common in north-east England?
(b) Suggest reasons for this.

G Questions

CASE STUDY OF NORTH-EAST ENGLAND

Look at Figure 8.5.

G1 Describe the main heavy industries in north-east England.

Look at Figure 8.8.

G2 Describe the distribution of heavy industries in north-east England.

Look at Figure 8.7.

G3 Suggest reasons why Teesside became important for steelmaking in the nineteenth century.
G4 Give one advantage and one disadvantage of steelmaking on Teesside today.

Look at Figure 8.10.

G5 What were the main reasons for the importance of shipbuilding in north-east England?
G6 What were the main reasons for the decline of shipbuilding?

Look at Figure 8.13.

G7 Do you think Teesside is a suitable location for the chemical industry? Give reasons for your answer.

Figure 8.4 Blyth Power Station.

CASE STUDY OF NORTH-EAST ENGLAND

Figure 8.5

Introduction

In the 1800s, north-east England changed from a farming region into an area of heavy industry. This was mainly due to the vast deposits of coal found underground and extending under the sea. The coal attracted steel, shipbuilding and heavy engineering industries, for which the area became world famous.

In the 1900s, these industries began to decline, while others started up, such as chemicals, oil refining and aluminium smelting.

Figure 8.6

Coal-mining

The north-east of England was the first part of Britain to mine coal. It was first mined from shallow pits 700 years ago and much of it was sent by sea to London. In the nineteenth century, when coal was needed for steam power in the new factories, hundreds of mines were dug all over the region, especially in Durham. Today, however, most of the coal has been **exhausted** (run out) and there are no deep mines left. All that remains are some **opencast** workings (where the coal is taken directly off the surface).

Figure 8.7

Iron and Steelmaking

The iron and steel industry became important in north-east England towards the end of the nineteenth century when high grade iron ore was found in the Cleveland Hills, south of the river Tees. With plenty of coal mined nearby, towns on Teesside, such as Middlesbrough, became centres of iron- and steelmaking. The industry prospered until the 1930s and then declined as local supplies of coal and iron ore ran out. Now there is only one steelworks open. It is on Teesside, where there is a large area of flat land, and the deep water of the Tees Estuary allows bulk carriers to import iron-ore.

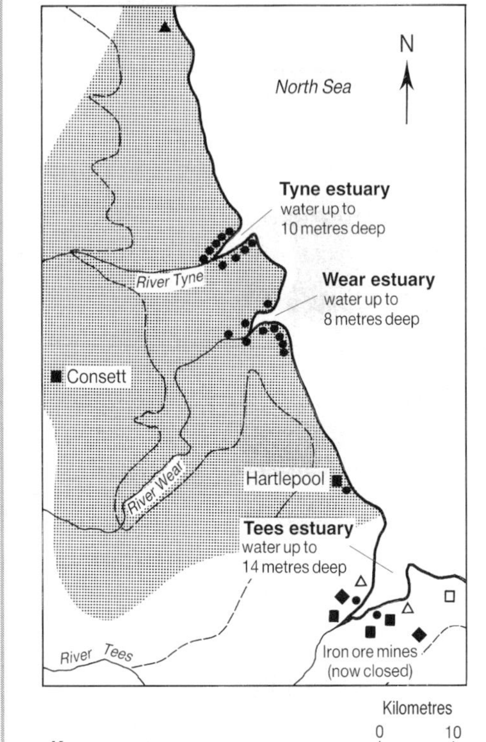

Figure 8.8 Heavy industry in north-east England

Figure 8.9 An old shipyard on Tyneside.

Figure 8.10

Shipbuilding

Ships were first built in the north-east to take coal to London. The industry grew when steam ships became popular in the nineteenth century. This was because there was plenty of coal and steel nearby and also deep sheltered water. The estuaries of the Tyne and Wear, around Newcastle and Sunderland, were lined with shipyards. But this industry also declined in the 1930s. Now there are no shipyards open. The last one, on the Tyne, closed in 1994. Once the local raw materials ran out, other countries, such as Japan, began to make ships more cheaply.

Figure 8.11

Power stations in North-east England

Location	Type of power station
Blyth	coal-fired
Blyth	wind-powered
Hartlepool	nuclear
Lynemouth	coal-fired
Teesside	gas-fired

Figure 8.12

The Chemical Industry

Although some chemicals were produced on Tyneside before 1900, the industry did not become important in this area until the company ICI set up a large works on Teesside in the 1920s. The factors that affected its location are shown in Figure 8.13.

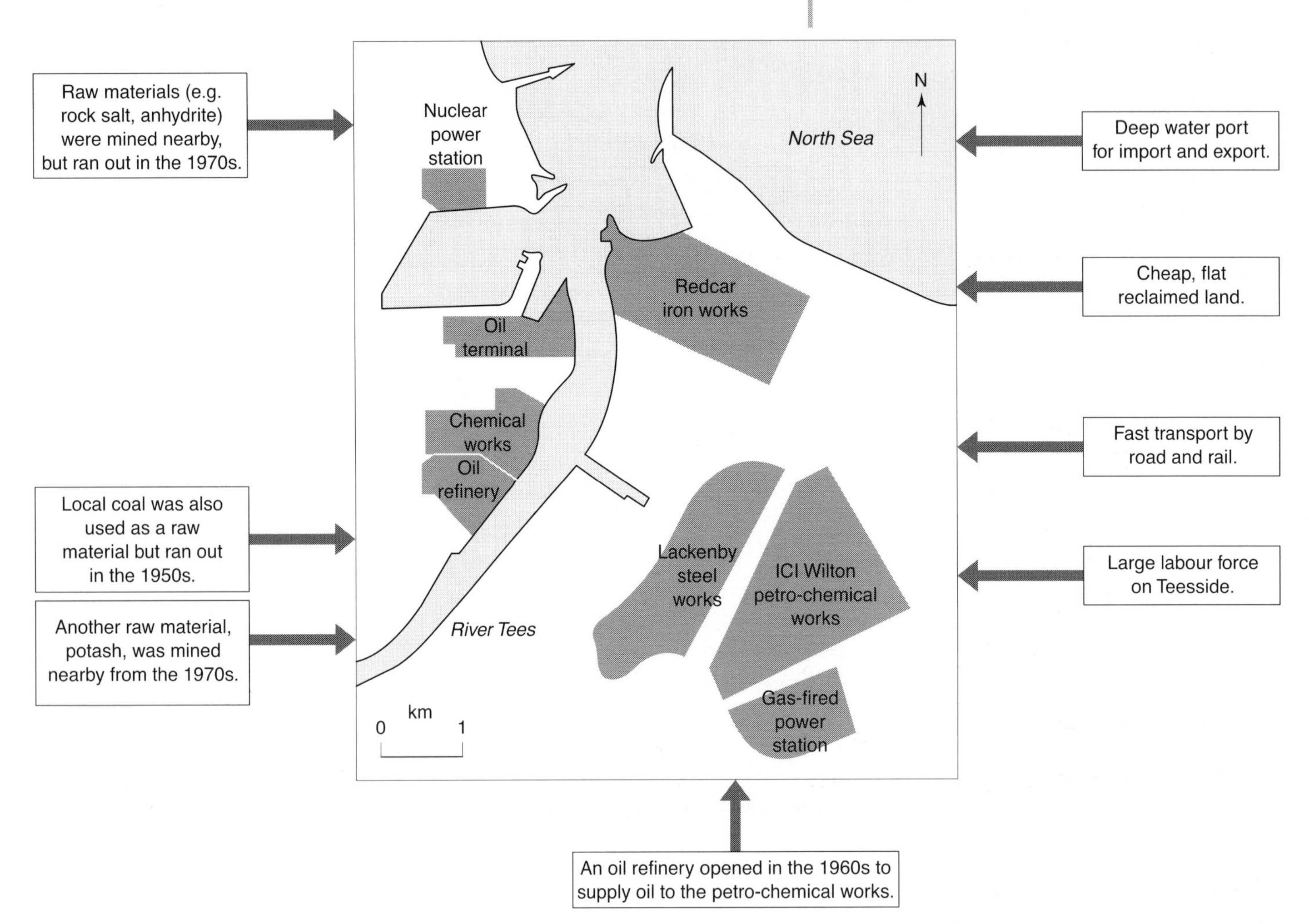

Figure 8.13 The chemical industry on Teesside.

Figure 8.14

The Aluminium Industry

The aluminium industry of north-east England is a modern heavy industry, dating from 1968. An aluminium smelter was built on flat land south of the village of Lynemouth, near to a coal-fired power station and a coal-mine. A railway separates the power station from the smelter and leads to the port of Blyth, 12 km to the south. It is through Blyth that the alumina for the smelter is imported.

Extension Text

8G CLASSIFICATION OF MANUFACTURING INDUSTRY

All manufacturing industries are either **heavy** or **light industries.** They are also either **processing** or **assembly** industries.

Processing industries change or process raw materials to produce a finished or semi-finished product, for example, steelmaking. Assembly industries collect or assemble manufactured items to produce finished goods, for example, shipbuilding.

Industries are also either **labour-intensive** or **capital-intensive**. Labour-intensive industries are those that use many workers but little machinery, such as pottery. Capital-intensive industries are those that use a lot of machinery but relatively few workers, such as power stations.

8H THE PULL OF RAW MATERIALS AND MARKETS

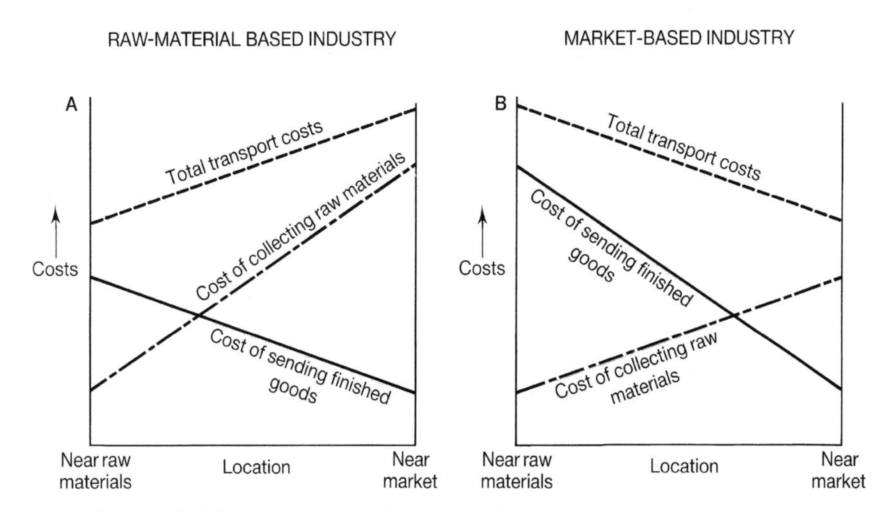

Figure 8.15 How cost affects the location of raw-material based industry and market-based industry.

A factory's raw materials and its market are usually in different locations. A company will choose to set up a factory near the source of its raw materials if it costs more to collect the raw materials than to distribute the finished goods (see Figure 8.15). This is common with heavy industries, where the raw materials are heavier than the finished goods. If it costs more to distribute the finished goods than to collect the raw materials, then the factory will be located near its market (see Figure 8.15). This is common with light industries.

8J THE ALUMINIUM INDUSTRY

The aluminium industry is a heavy, capital-intensive, processing industry. Aluminium is made from bauxite, a rock not found in Britain. Aluminium is made in two stages:

1 The bauxite is heated to separate it from the waste rock. This produces alumina. Ten tonnes of bauxite are needed to make 4

tonnes of alumina. Because the cost of collecting 10 tonnes of bauxite is greater than the cost of distributing 4 tonnes of alumina, this stage of the industry is located near the raw material. The nearest location to imported raw materials is in ports.

2 Smelting converts the alumina into aluminium, using huge amounts of electricity. Four tonnes of alumina and 15 000 kWh of electricity are needed to make one tonne of aluminium. Because the biggest cost is power, aluminium smelters are located near a cheap supply of electricity. The most common location is near a hydro-electric power station, where prices are slightly cheaper than elsewhere.

E Questions

Read the Extension Text.

E1 In the brewing industry, one tonne of raw material is used to make 5 tonnes of beer. Is the brewing industry a market-based or raw-material based industry?

E2 Explain why the production of alumina in Britain takes place in or near ports.

C Questions

CASE STUDY OF NORTH-EAST ENGLAND

Look at Figure 8.8.

C1 Describe the changing location of heavy industry in north-east England.

Look at Figures 8.7, 8.10 and 8.14.

C2 What were the main factors in the location of (a) steelworks, (b) shipyards and (c) aluminium smelters in north-east England?

C3 In what ways are the coal, steel and shipbuilding industries of north-east England connected?

Look at Figures 8.11, 8.13 and 8.14.

C4 Suggest reasons for the types of power stations found in north-east England.

Look at Figure 8.13.

C5 Describe the advantages and disadvantages of making chemicals on Teesside today.

UNIT 9

Light Industry

Core Text

9A LIGHT INDUSTRY

A **light industry** is a manufacturing industry that uses light, raw materials in small amounts to produce light or small goods such as watches or television sets.

9B LOCATION OF LIGHT INDUSTRIES

Light industries are set up in locations where they are:

1. **Near fast transport** – most light industries use a number of raw materials which come from different areas. They need to be beside main roads so that raw materials can be brought in cheaply and quickly, and finished goods can be delivered to customers rapidly.
2. **Near to market** – their raw materials are light and can be moved long distances cheaply. As a result, many light industries set up near their market. If they sell their goods to the public, their biggest market is in cities.
3. **Near a labour supply** – many light industries need skilled workers. These industries set up where a skilled labour force can be found.
4. **Offered government aid** – the government and the European Union encourage industries to set up in certain areas of the country by offering them aid. If a company has a choice of locations, it will often choose an area where this regional aid is available.

9C INDUSTRIAL ESTATES

Many light industries are located on **industrial estates** or **business parks**. These are planned areas in towns and cities where only factories and offices can be built. Most are found at the edges of towns or in inner-city areas that are being redeveloped. To attract companies, industrial estates need to be located:

- close to fast communications, especially main roads
- on cheap, flat land
- where there is room to expand.

9D REGIONAL AID

The government wants more industries to set up in areas of high unemployment, and attracts industries by:

- **giving grants and loans** to factories that set up in the area
- **building more roads** to serve the area
- **training the local labour force** in the skills required
- **offering low rents and rates** for the first few years
- **providing ready-made factories** with services laid on.

Areas where the government offers some help to industry are called **Assisted Areas**. Smaller areas where the government offers a great deal of help to industry are called **Enterprise Zones**.

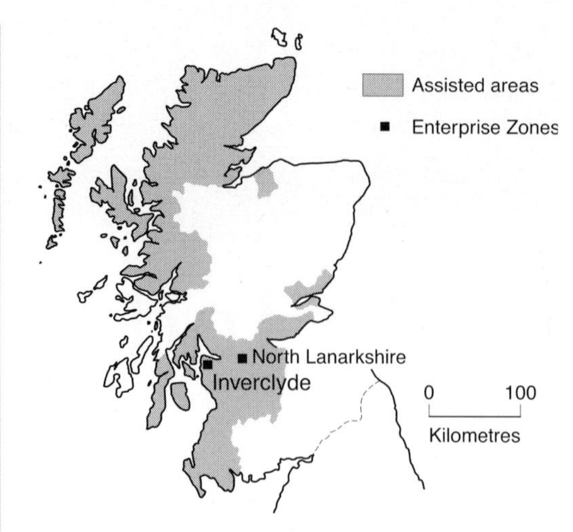

Figure 9.1 Assisted Areas in Scotland.

9E THE ELECTRONICS INDUSTRY

The electronics industry is an example of a **high-technology industry**. The industry makes electronic equipment, for example computers, video recorders and microwave ovens, most of which use microchips – tiny chips of silica in which thousands of bits of information can be stored.

The electronics industry locates:

1. **near skilled labour** – often close to universities, in order to use the highly qualified people there and to keep in touch with new research
2. **near main roads and airports** – fast transport is important and most of the raw materials are so light they can be sent by air
3. **where there is regional aid** – because there are so many suitable places to set up, the industry sometimes chooses a place where there is regional aid
4. **in an attractive environment** – to attract the highly skilled people it needs.

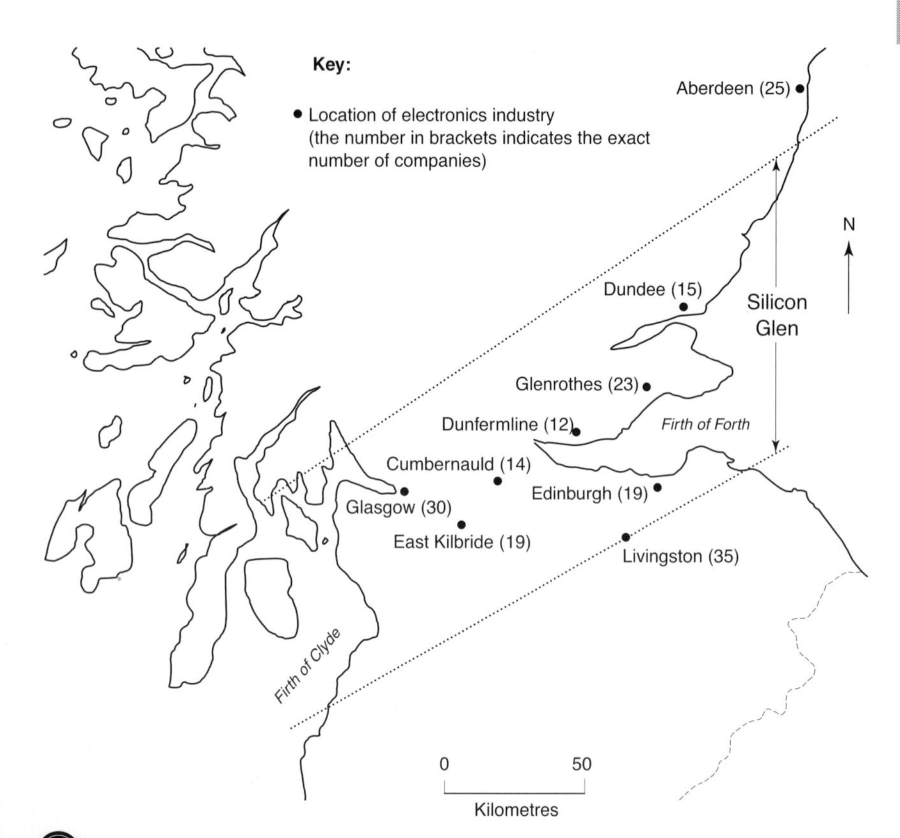

Figure 9.2 The location of electronics companies in Scotland.

In Scotland, most electronics companies have set up in the Central Lowlands (known as Silicon Glen), especially in the big cities and new towns. These areas have (or have had) regional aid. There are also many universities nearby, as well as motorways, airports and a large pool of skilled labour.

9F THE VEHICLE INDUSTRY

Location 1

Between 1900 and 1960 the vehicle industry was located in the West Midlands (e.g. Coventry) and south-east England (e.g. Dagenham). These areas were chosen because they:

- **were near skilled labour** – in engineering and metal working.
- **were near the market** – most people live in the south of England.
- **had good communications** – by 1960 cars were made from over 1000 components brought in by road and rail from all parts of the country.

Location 2

After 1960, the vehicle industry was located in Assisted Areas in Scotland, England and Wales (although some have now closed). These areas were chosen because:

- **regional aid was available** – car works were attracted to areas of high unemployment because of regional aid.
- **they had good communications** – near main roads and railways.

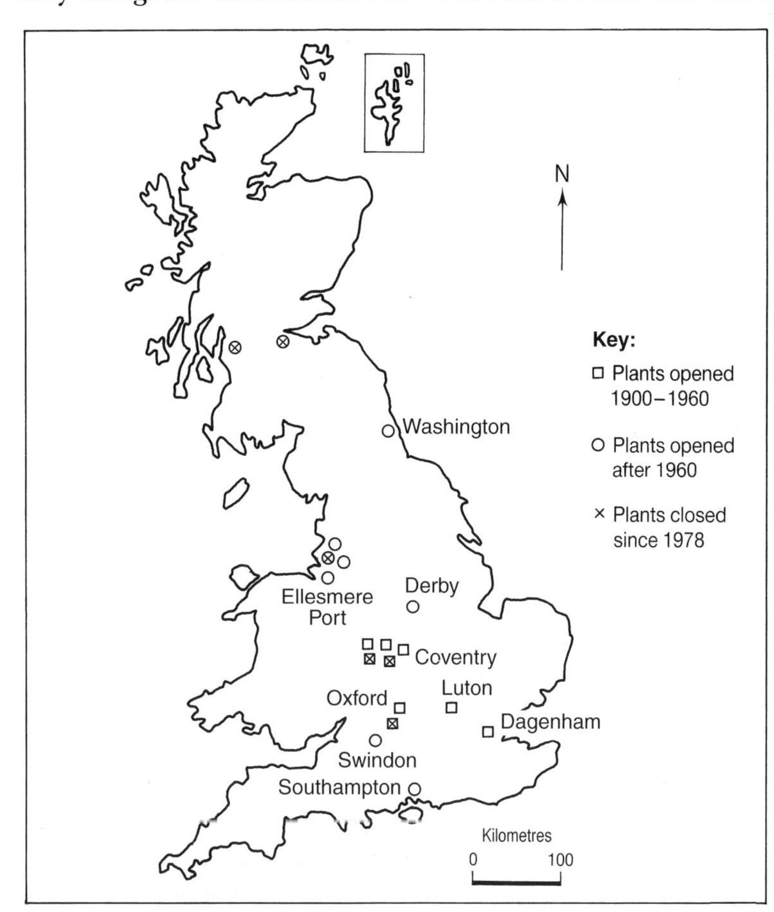

Figure 9.3 The locations of the vehicle industry since 1900.

Core Questions

Look at 9B.

1 Which of the following factors are important to light industries: nearness to raw materials, nearness to market, nearness to power supply, good communications, nearness to workers, regional aid?

Look at 9C.

2 What are industrial estates?
3 What is another name for an industrial estate?

Look at 9D.

4 Describe three ways in which the government can attract companies to an area.
5 Why does the government do this?
6 What is the difference between Assisted Areas and Enterprise Zones?

Look at Figure 9.1.

7 Name two Enterprise Zones in Scotland.

Look at 9E.

8 Why do electronics companies sometimes set up near universities?
9 Why do you think Central Scotland is called 'Silicon Glen'?

Look at 9F.

10 Why does the vehicle industry need good communications?

Look at Figure 9.3.

11 Name three car plants in Britain that have opened since 1960.

F Questions

CASE STUDY OF THE THAMES CORRIDOR

Look at Figure 9.5.

F1 Where is the Thames Corridor?
F2 What types of industry have set up in the Thames Corridor in the last 25 years?

Look at Figure 9.7.

F3 What are the two main reasons why the electronics industry came to the Thames Corridor?

Look at Figure 9.15.

F4 What are the main reasons the car industry set up (a) at Oxford in 1912 and (b) at Swindon in 1985?

Look at Figures 9.13 and 9.14.

F5 (a) What are the main types of industry at Oxford Business Park?
(b) Do you think this is a suitable location for a business park? Give reasons for your answer.

Figure 9.4 The Honda car plant in Swindon.

Look at Figures 9.10 and 9.11.

F6 What are the main types of industry at Oxford Science Park?

F7 Why do you think companies want to set up at this science park?

G Questions

CASE STUDY OF THE THAMES CORRIDOR

Look at Figure 9.5.

G1 Describe the location of the Thames Corridor.

G2 What are the advantages of the Thames Corridor for light industry?

Look at Figure 9.7.

G3 Do you think electronics companies set up in the Thames Corridor chiefly because of the good communications? Give reasons for your answer.

Look at Figures 9.11 and 9.14.

G4 Compare the types of industry at Oxford Business Park and Oxford Science Park.

Look at Figure 9.13.

G5 Describe the attractions of Oxford Business Park for light industry.

Look at Figure 9.15.

G6 What have been the most important factors encouraging the car industry to set up in Swindon?

Look at Figure 9.16.

G7 Describe the main characteristics of just-in-time (JIT) production.

CASE STUDY OF THE THAMES CORRIDOR

Figure 9.5

Introduction

The Thames Corridor is a triangular area west of London, between the M4 and M40 motorways. It is shown in Figure 9.5. It is a lowland area, surrounded by low, chalk hills, and includes the university towns of Oxford and Reading. In the last 25 years, a great number of light industries have set up in the Thames Corridor, especially high-technology companies.

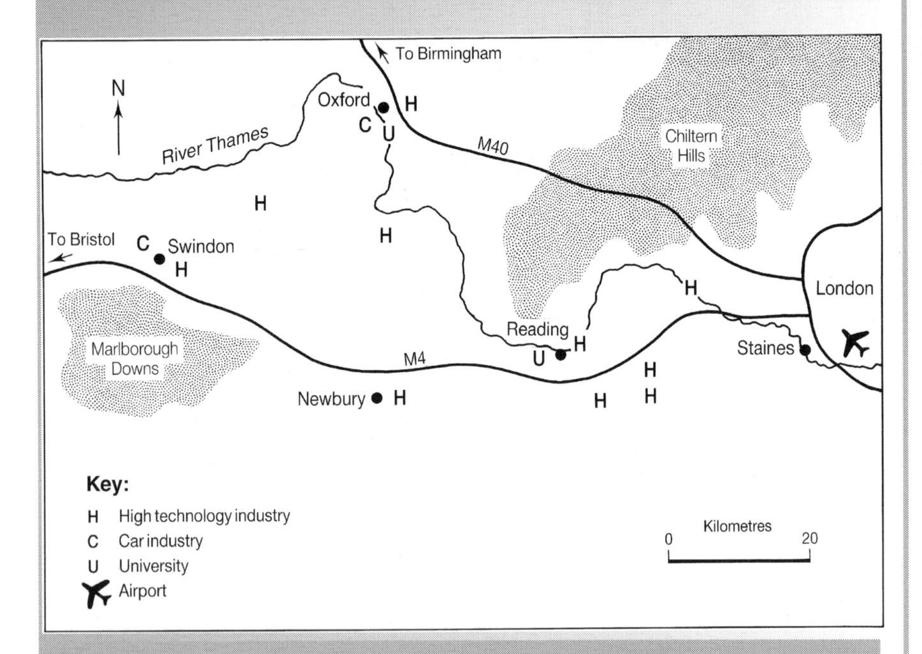

Figure 9.6 The Thames Corridor.

Figure 9.7

The Electronics Industry

The Thames Corridor is one of the most important areas in the UK for electronics. A wide range of goods are researched, designed and made here, including semi-conductors, telecommunications equipment and computers. Companies set up here because:

1 the M4 and M40 motorways are nearby, which means that goods can be brought in and sent out very quickly
2 Heathrow Airport is close by, making it easy for managers to travel to their company headquarters overseas
3 there is a highly skilled workforce due, at first, to the many research centres that were already in the area (e.g. aircraft research, nuclear weapons research)
4 companies can use the facilities of nearby universities
5 the area is surrounded by attractive countryside, such as the Chiltern Hills.

Figure 9.8

Other High-technology Industries

The Thames Corridor has other high-technology industries, including pharmaceuticals (drugs), biotechnology, aerospace, defence and information technology. Some of these have located at science parks, such as Oxford Science Park, shown in Figure 9.10.

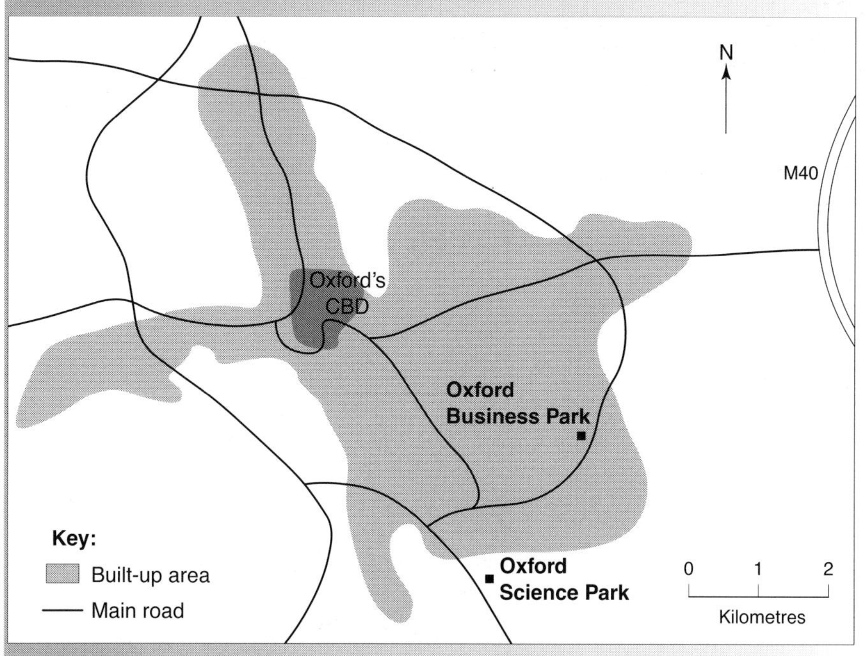

Figure 9.9 The locations of Oxford Science Park and Oxford Business Park.

Figure 9.10 Oxford Science Park.

Figure 9.11 Oxford Science Park	
Manufacturing industries	
pharmaceuticals	4
electronics	16
medical	5
Service industries	
consultancy	8
information technology	3
research and development	4
others	2

Figure 9.12

Other Light Industries

As well as high-technology industries, the Thames Corridor can boast a wide range of other light industries. These have set up in the area because of the fast communications and the large market in nearby London and south-east England. Many companies have set up at business parks, such as Oxford Business Park, shown in Figure 9.13.

Figure 9.13 Oxford Business Park.

Figure 9.14 Oxford Business Park	
Manufacturing industries	
(including a chemical company and a publishing company)	4
Service industries	
offices	4
information technology	2
banks	2
hotel	1
warehouse	1
others	2

Figure 9.15

The Car Industry

An older example of a light industry in the Thames Corridor area is the car industry. Cars have been made at Cowley, Oxford, since 1912. The industry located there because there was a large labour force nearby, as well as good road and rail links, making it easy to bring in components and send out finished cars. Cheap land was also available.

In 1985, the Japanese firm of Honda built a car assembly plant at Swindon. They were attracted by the local workforce that was skilled in engineering because Swindon originally grew up as a centre for making locomotive engines. The excellent communications, by motorway, to ports and airports was important, as was the availability of a large greenfield site.

Figure 9.16

Car Assembly Methods

The car industry is an assembly industry. The different components, such as doors, engines and windscreens, are made elsewhere and assembled on an assembly line. Until recently, car companies stored several weeks' supplies of components at their assembly plants. Now, companies like Honda bring in their components only when they are needed. This is called **just-in-time (JIT) production**. It saves the company the cost of storing components and it means they do not need such a large factory. With JIT methods, it is important that the assembly plant gets the components it needs very quickly and reliably.

Extension Text

9G HEAVY AND LIGHT INDUSTRIES

Heavy industries are usually 'tied' to their raw materials. A site near a source of raw materials is the cheapest location for them. But light industries' costs do not vary much from one location to another. They are called **footloose** or **mobile industries**.

Most of Britain's heavy industries date from the nineteenth century and are now in decline. They are called **sunset** or **smokestack industries**. Many light industries are new and growing in importance. They are called **sunrise industries**.

9H SCIENCE PARKS

Sunrise, high-technology light industries usually locate in business parks. **Science parks** are reserved for companies that are involved in research. They are located near to universities and have links with them. Like most business parks, science parks are sited on land which has not previously been built on. These areas are called **greenfield sites**. Because high-technology industries need to attract highly skilled workers, who are in short supply, they usually locate in attractive environments, often near motorway junctions so workers can easily get to work.

9J ASSEMBLY INDUSTRIES

Many light industries use **assembly line methods** to **mass produce** their goods. Instead of one skilled person making the whole product, the different operations are done by semi-skilled workers along an assembly line. By specialising in one operation, each person works more quickly. This increases **productivity** (number of products made in a given time), although the jobs are very repetitive.

9K SUMMARY OF LOCATION FACTORS

In unit 7, the seven main factors in the location of industry were described. Studies of specific industries in units 8 and 9 have shown that other factors may also be important. All these factors are shown in Figure 9.17.

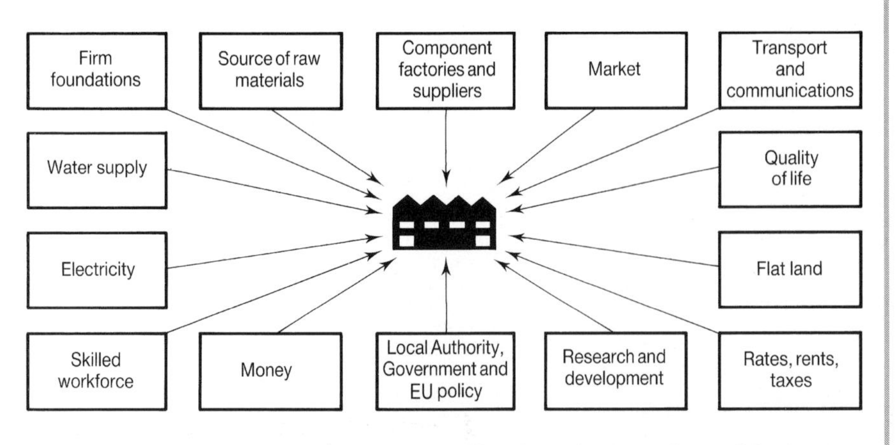

Figure 9.17 Factors affecting the location of industry.

E Questions

Read the Extension Text.

E1 Which of the following industries are examples of sunrise industries: electronics, bakeries, shipbuilding, pharmaceuticals (making drugs), steelmaking?

E2 Why are light industries called footloose industries?

E3 Which factors are important in the location of science parks?

E4 What are the benefits of assembly-line production?

E5 What is a greenfield site?

C Questions

CASE STUDY OF THE THAMES CORRIDOR

Look at Figure 9.7.

C1 What are the main reasons for the growth of the electronics industry in the Thames Corridor?

Look at Figures 9.10, 9.11, 9.13 and 9.14.

C2 What are the similarities and differences between Oxford Science Park and Oxford Business Park?

Look at Figure 9.15.

C3 Compare the factors in the location of a car works in Oxford in the early 1900s and in Swindon in the 1980s.

Look at Figure 9.16.

C4 What are the main advantages and disadvantages of JIT production to car companies?

C5 Do you think that JIT methods will affect the location of car component industries? Give reasons for your answer.

UNIT 10

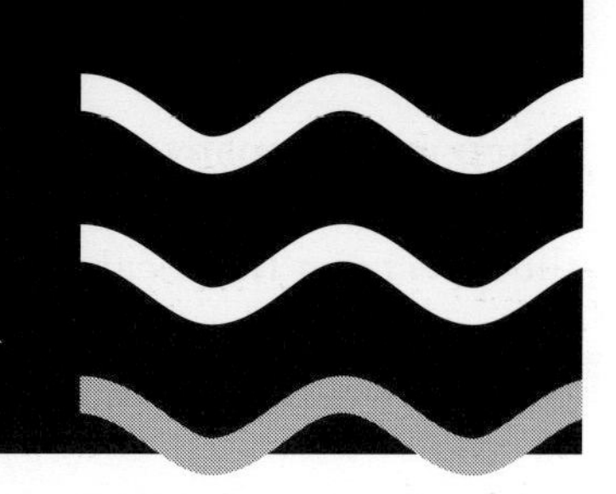

The Changing Location of Industry

Core Text

10A CHANGES IN INDUSTRY

We have already found out that there are two types of manufacturing industry – heavy and light industry – and that they prefer to set up in different locations. We have also found out that many of Britain's heavy industries are old and in decline, while many light industries are new and growing. This means that many industries are closing down in old, heavy industrial areas. Meanwhile, in new, light industrial areas, industries are opening and expanding.

When industries set up in a new area or when they close down, they affect their local areas in many ways.

10B EFFECTS OF NEW INDUSTRIES

When a new factory is built, it brings many jobs, not just in the factory itself. First, people are needed to build the factory. Then, once it starts up, it may use local tradespeople and transport companies. With extra jobs, the population may rise, so new houses will be built. Shops and other services will do more trade, because there are more people with more money to spend. On the downside, the amount of traffic in the area will probably increase and there may be more noise and air pollution.

10C EFFECTS OF FACTORIES CLOSING

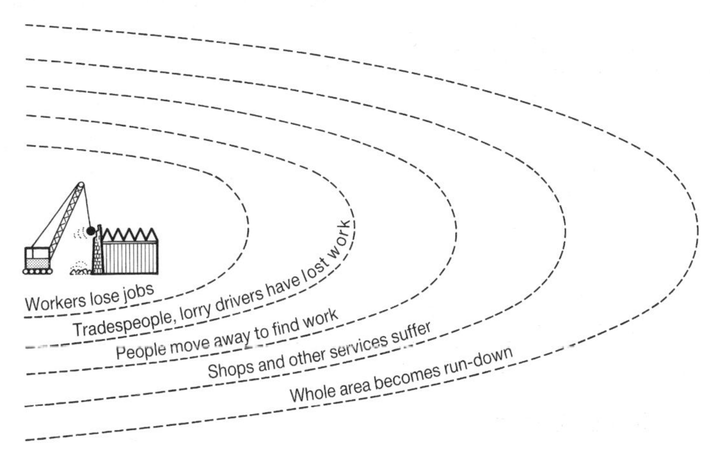

Figure 10.1 The effects of a factory closing down.

When any company closes down, people become unemployed. But, if a large factory that employs most of the people in the area shuts, the effects on the local community can be very severe.

10D THE COAL-MINING INDUSTRY

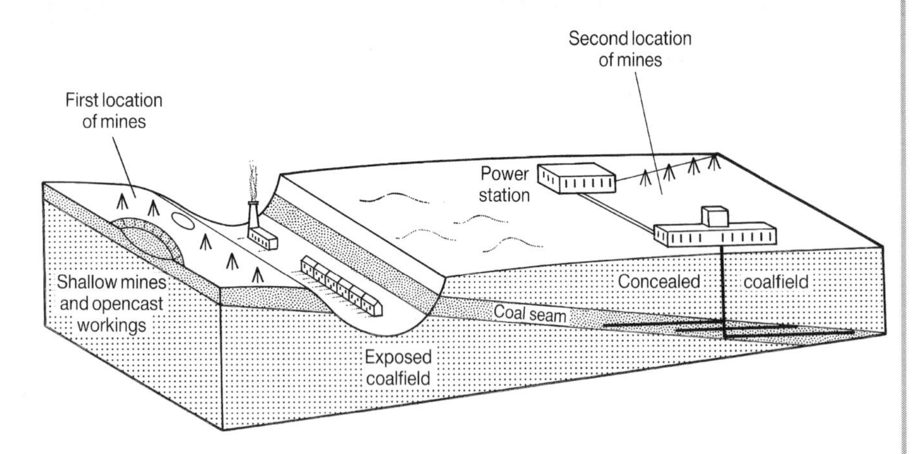

Figure 10.2 Changes in the location of coal mines.

For the last 200 years, coal-mining has been one of the most important industries in the UK. Coal was needed in the nineteenth century, especially to produce steam power for factories and trains. In the twentieth century, coal has been much needed in power stations. Many mines were dug in the nineteenth century and all the coal was removed. More mines were opened in the twentieth century, but in different locations.

- **Location 1:** at **exposed coalfields**, coal seams are near the surface and many shallow mines and **opencast** workings take coal off the surface.
- **Location 2:** when the exposed coal runs out, new mines open in the **concealed coalfield**. Deep shafts have to be dug down to the coal seams. Many of these mines have now closed as the coal has run out or become too expensive to extract.

10E EFFECTS OF COAL-MINE CLOSURES

Most coal mines in the UK were located in small settlements. When the mines closed, the local areas were very badly affected. The effects can be in three stages:

1 unemployment rises, people move away, shops close and the area becomes **derelict**, with disused railway lines, waste tips, etc.
2 with high unemployment in the area, regional aid is given to restore the landscape (for example, pulling down old buildings, landscaping waste tips) so that it can be used again.
3 aid is given to new factories that set up in the area. As new industries open, peoples' standard of living should start to rise again.

10F PORTS

Many of our industries have relied on importing raw materials and exporting finished goods. Most of this trade has taken place in ports. The location of ports, however, has changed in the last 200 years.

- **Location 1** Before 1800, ports were located in sheltered, tidal water, often in river estuaries a little way upstream, near the largest settlement.
- **Location 2** Between 1800 and 1950, docks were built downstream in deeper water for larger ships to use.
- **Location 3** Since 1950, new jetties and terminals have been built in the deepest water well downstream, for very large ships.

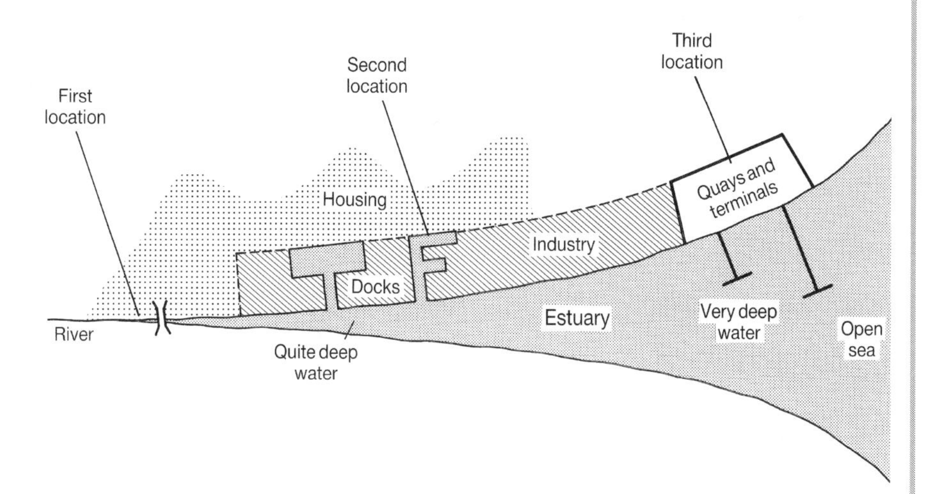

Figure 10.3 Changes in the location of port activity.

10G EFFECTS OF DOCKS CLOSING

As ports have moved downstream and the nineteenth-century docks have closed, nearby areas have been severely affected. The effects can be in three stages:

1. unemployment rises as docks, nearby factories and warehouses close down, and the area becomes derelict.
2. with high unemployment, the area receives regional aid to **redevelop** (for example, fill in the old docks, build new houses, industrial estates, marinas and roads).
3. once the area is more attractive, aid is then given to bring in new businesses. As these open, standards of living should rise.

Figure 10.4 The redevelopment of Liverpool's docks.

Core Questions

Look at 10A.

1. In which areas are many industries closing down?
2. In which areas are many industries opening?

Look at Figure 10.1.

3. Which of the following are likely to happen when a large factory closes?
   (a) unemployment increases

(b) the population rises
(c) shops do less business
(d) the area becomes run down

Look at 10B.

4 When a new factory opens:
(a) why do shops do more trade?
(b) in what way will local tradespeople be affected?
(c) why are more houses often built?

Look at 10D.

5 What name is given to a coalfield where the coal is close to the surface?
6 Give one reason why coal mines have to close.

Look at 10E.

7 Many old coal-mining areas have become derelict. What does this mean?

Look at 10F.

8 Why have many ports moved to deeper water?

Look at 10G.

9 Many old dock areas have been redeveloped. What does this mean?

F Questions

CASE STUDY OF NORTH-EAST ENGLAND

Look at Figure 10.8.

F1 How has the number of coal mines in north-east England changed since 1957?

Look at Figure 10.10.

F2 In 1981, Blackhall Colliery was closed.
(a) Why do you think some of the shops there have since closed?
(b) Why do you think there are fewer children in the village now?

Look at Figure 10.12.

F3 How has the number of steelworks in north-east England changed since 1950?

Look at Figure 10.10.

F4 Why did unemployment in the town of Consett rise to 26% in 1981?
F5 In the 1980s, Consett received a lot of money from the government. How was this money spent?
F6 In what ways have conditions in Consett improved since 1981?

Look at Figure 10.14.

F7 Why do you think it is important for companies to be given grants to set up in north-east England?

Look at Figure 10.15.

F8 In what ways has the opening of the Nissan car plant helped people in north-east England?

G Questions

CASE STUDY OF NORTH-EAST ENGLAND

Look at Figure 10.8.

G1 Describe the changes in coal-mining since 1957.

Look at Figure 10.6.

G2 Describe the effects of the closure of Blackhall Colliery in 1981.

Look at Figure 10.10.

G3 Suggest why the closure of Consett steelworks affected the town so badly.
G4 What evidence is there that Consett has now recovered from the closure of the steelworks?

Look at Figures 10.11 and 10.13.

G5 Describe the changes in the shipbuilding industry since 1957.

Look at Figure 10.14.

G6 Which has been more important in attracting new industries to north-east England – restoring derelict land, or improving the road system? Give reasons for your answer.

Look at Figure 10.15 and the statement below.

G7 Do you agree with the statement below? Give reasons for your answer.
'Nissan employs 4100 people. That is not helping the north-east very much.' (local councillor)

CASE STUDY OF NORTH-EAST ENGLAND

Figure 10.5

Introduction

Unit 7 looked at the growth of heavy industry in north-east England in the nineteenth century. We learned that many of these industries have declined in the last 50 years, especially coal-mining, steelmaking and shipbuilding. More recently, new light industries have set up in the region. The effects of this will now be studied in detail.

Figure 10.6

The Decline of Coal-Mining

Figure 10.8 shows the rapid decline of coal-mining in north-east England since the 1950s.

Most of the coal used to be mined in small 'pit villages' and a typical pit village is Blackhall Colliery. There was no village in Blackhall until 1909, when the mine opened and rows of terraced houses were built. By the 1930s, 6000 people worked in the pit and 90 per cent of the jobs in the village were connected with the pit. Many shops and services opened up and, by 1980, there were over 50 shops, three churches and two primary schools. But in 1981 the mine closed, as did other mines in the local area. There were few other jobs. Miners were given the choice of early retirement or transfer to a mine in another area. Today, some shops are empty, many houses are for sale and one of the primary schools has closed.

Figure 10.8

Year	Number of people employed in coal-mining	Number of mines
1957	168 000	105
1967	113 000	49
1977	40 000	26
1987	25 000	7
1997	0	0

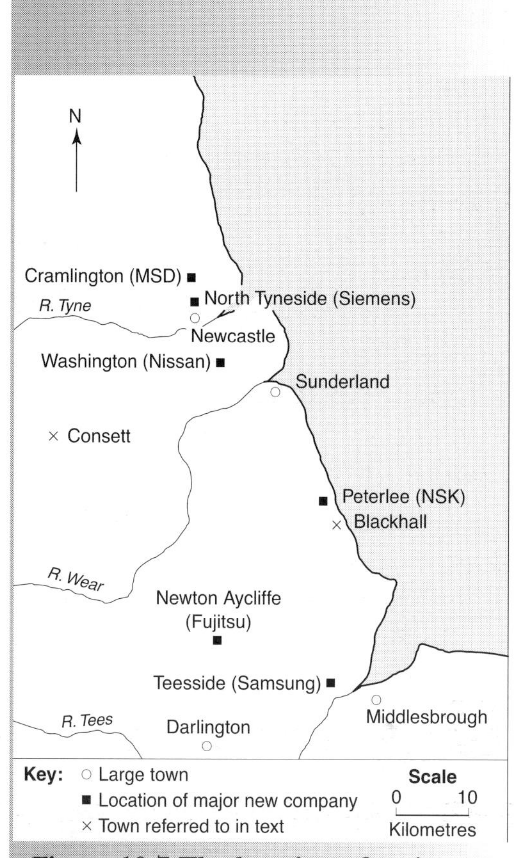

Figure 10.7 The location of major new companies in north-east England.

Figure 10.9 Terrace of houses in Blackhall.

Figure 10.10

The Decline of Steelmaking

Although steel is still made at Redcar on Teesside, this industry has also declined, as Figure 10.12 shows.

The small town of Consett was badly affected when its steelworks closed in 1980.

Consett in 1980

- over 3000 steelworkers unemployed (total population: 30 000)
- unemployment rises to 26%
- population begins to fall
- large areas of derelict land
- £11 million needed to demolish steelworks and restore site
- £13 million needed to improve roads and the environment
- £17 million needed to build new industrial estates

Consett in 1997

- £35 million in grants received from the government and the European Union
- over 5000 new jobs created
- more than 200 companies attracted to Consett
- 10 industrial estates set up
- population increasing

Figure 10.11

Year	Number of people employed in shipbuilding	Number of shipyards
1957	65 000	40
1967	45 000	27
1977	37 000	10
1987	17 000	2
1997	0	0

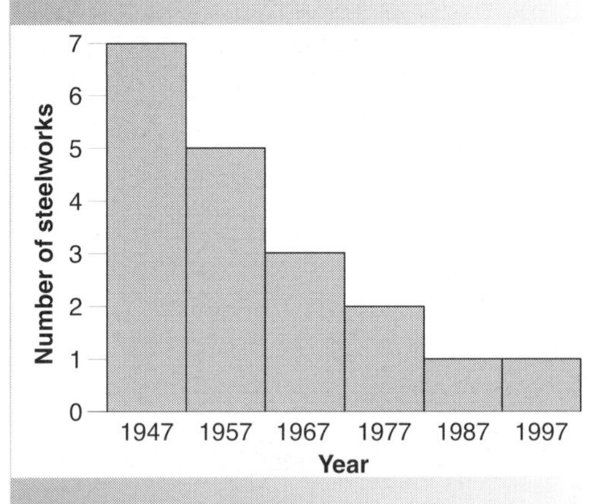

Figure 10.12 The number of steelworks in north-east England since 1947.

Figure 10.13

The Decline of Shipbuilding

As recently as the early 1980s, north-east England was the most important shipbuilding area in the UK, but now no ships are built here. The last shipyard, Swan Hunter of Tyneside, closed in 1995 and 3000 workers lost their jobs.

Figure 10.14

The Rise of New Light Industries

Between 1970 and 1985, the north-east lost over 100 000 jobs in manufacturing industry. Since then, the area has attracted many new industries, often run by foreign companies. It has done this by:

1 setting up **Urban Development Corporations** on Tyneside, Wearside and Teesside, to restore derelict land and make attractive sites for industry
2 improving many roads to motorway standard and developing local airports
3 giving government grants to persuade companies to set up in the north-east; for example, Nissan was given £100 million, Samsung £58 million and Siemens £30 million.

Figure 10.15

The Nissan Car Works, Sunderland

The biggest company to move to the north-east is Nissan. It opened a car assembly plant on a greenfield site near Sunderland in 1984. It has benefitted the area in many ways:

- it provides 4100 jobs
- 25 component suppliers have also moved to the north-east, employing a further 6000 people
- other Japanese companies have since set up in the UK
- its success has attracted other big companies, like Samsung, Siemens, Fujitsu and Lucky Goldstar. By 1997, 400 foreign companies had sites in the north-east.

Extension Text

10H EFFECTS OF FACTORY CLOSURES

The closure of a large factory has wide-ranging effects, both locally and nationally:

1 **Economic Effects**
Workers at the factory become unemployed, and nearby industries that depended on the factory may also close or have to lay off workers. With less money, people spend less locally at, for example, shops, cinemas and garages. These businesses also suffer. The Council receives less rates, leaving it with less money to spend on improving the area. New industries are also reluctant to set up in such a run-down area.

2 **Social Effects**
Unemployment lowers people's standard of living. The sense of hopelessness that unemployment often brings may also contribute to the break-up of families and an increase in crime. Young people often move away to find work elsewhere, leaving behind mostly older people in the run-down community.

3 **Environmental Effects**
The disused factories, canals, railways and mines become derelict. Some of the houses, blackened by years of factory smoke, lay empty. Waste tips and polluted rivers contribute to the atmosphere of decay and depression.

10J EFFECTS OF NEW FACTORIES

The opening of a new factory has the opposite effects of a factory closure. The extra work and wealth spreads throughout the whole community. This is called the **multiplier effect**.

10K THE PATTERN OF ECONOMIC CHANGE

More factories have closed in the old, heavy industrial areas of the UK, while more factories have opened in the new, light industrial areas. This has led to wide differences in standards of living throughout the country, as shown in Figure 10.16.

Figure 10.16 Differences in living standards within the UK

Economic region	Unemployment (%) (1994)	Average weekly income (£) (1994)	Population change (%) (1981–94)
England			
North	11	285	+1
North West	10	317	0
Yorkshire and Humberside	9	303	+4
West Midlands	9	304	+4
East Midlands	7	344	+8
East Anglia	6	350	+14
South West	7	346	+13
South East	7	407	+8
Wales	9	295	+6
Scotland	10	314	+2
Northern Ireland	16	281	+7

Read the Extension Text.

E1 Describe three economic and three social effects of a factory closure.

E2 In what ways do factory closures affect the environment?

E3 What is the multiplier effect?

Look at Figure 10.16.

E4 Rank the economic regions of the UK according to each of the indicators of standard of living.

E5 Which region has (a) the highest overall rankings and (b) the lowest overall rankings?

C Questions

CASE STUDY OF NORTH-EAST ENGLAND

Look at Figure 10.6.

C1 Describe the social and environmental effects of the closure of the mine at Blackhall Colliery in 1981.

Look at Figure 10.10.

C2 Why do you think it was difficult to attract industry to Consett when the steelworks first closed?

C3 Describe the different arguments for and against the following point of view. 'The closure of the steelworks was the best thing to happen to Consett.' (local resident, 1997)

Look at Figure 10.14.

C4 Suggest reasons why light industry was attracted to north-east England in the 1980s and 1990s.

Look at Figure 10.15.

C5 Describe the multiplier effect on north-east England of the opening of the Nissan car works.

UNIT 11

Skills in Rural Studies

Core Text

11A INTRODUCTION TO RURAL STUDIES

Geography studies the land (the physical landscape) and the ways it is used (the human landscape). Over the whole of Britain, more land is used for farming than anything else. So, the study of farming and the countryside – called **rural studies** – has to be an important part of Geography.

For the Standard Grade examination, you need to know and understand the following:

1 arable, pastoral and mixed farming in the UK – their inputs, processes and outputs
2 the ways in which the physical landscape affects farming
3 the influence of the government and European Union on farming
4 recent changes in farming and the countryside in the UK
5 other land uses in the countryside, for example, recreation, forestry and quarrying
6 the benefits and problems that different land uses bring to an area.

You also need to develop the following enquiry skills:

1 how to gather information on the countryside, by interviewing people
2 how to process information, by drawing line graphs.

11B GATHERING INFORMATION

Different techniques can be used to gather information about the countryside. To find out about the topics covered in units 12–14, you might use some of the following techniques.

Figure 11.1

Topic studied	Gathering technique
Land uses in the countryside	**extracting information from maps** on farming, forestry, settlement **observing and recording** land uses by doing a survey **fieldsketching**

Figure 11.1 continued

Topic studied	Gathering technique
Farm inputs and outputs	**interviewing** farmers
Land-use changes	**observing and recording** land uses **extracting information from old maps** to find out land uses in the past **interviewing** local people
Land-use conflicts	**extracting information** from local newspapers **interviewing** people affected

11C PREPARING AN INTERVIEW

The best way of finding out information about a farm is to interview the farmer.

- Arrange the interview in advance, by letter or by phone.
- Tell the person the reason for the interview.
- Prepare the questions beforehand and write them down on a recording sheet, leaving plenty of space for answers.
- Do not ask unnecessary questions – the questions you ask should allow you to find out what you want to know. For example, for the interview shown in the following table, there is no need to ask the farmer how many workers he has or what jobs he does each month, as these are not relevant.
- The questions should allow you to obtain detailed information. For example, for the interview shown in Figure 11.2, if you just ask the farmer why he grows crops on his farm, you might receive a vague or incomplete answer, so ask him about all the aspects of his land which you know should affect what he does.
- At the end of the interview, thank the person for his/her help.

Figure 11.2

Interview Recording Sheet

Person interviewed: Bob Miles
Date of interview: 5 February 1998
Name of farm: Mearns Farm, Gargunnock
Aim: to explain the land uses on Mearns Farm

1. Which crops do you grow? ______________________

____

2. What area does each crop cover? ______________________

____

3. How many animals do you keep? ______________________

____

4. Does the soil quality affect what you grow? ______________________

____

____

5. Does the drainage affect what you grow? ______________________

______________________ ▶

Figure 11.2 continued

Interview Recording Sheet

6. Does the relief of your land affect you? ____________________

____

____

7. In what ways does the temperature here affect what you do?

____

____

8. In what ways does the rainfall affect what you do? __________

____

____

9. Is the fact that you are near a large town important? ________

____

____

11D DRAWING A LINE GRAPH

A **line graph** should be used to show how a quantity changes over time or distance.

- Plot time or distance on the horizontal (x) axis. For example, in Figure 11.3, the x axis shows years.
- The vertical (y) axis should show quantity. For example, in Figure 11.3, the y axis shows the number of workers.
- Draw the axes in pencil.
- Find the highest and lowest values on the x and y axes and then choose a suitable scale for each axis.
- Label the axes in pen, including the units.
- Plot each point carefully, in pencil, with a small cross.
- Join the crosses with a pencil line.
- Once you have checked your graph, go over the pencil lines in pen.
- Give the graph a title.

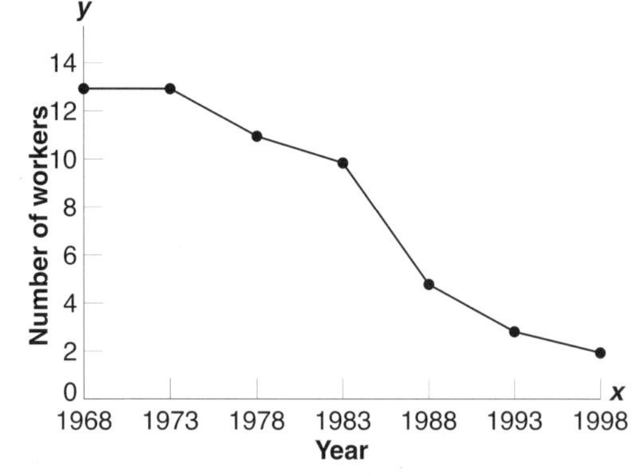

Figure 11.3 A line graph showing workers on Hillfoot Farm, Fife (1968–98).

11E DRAWING A MULTIPLE-LINE GRAPH

A multiple-line graph is when two or more line graphs are drawn on a single diagram. It is used to compare changes in two or more measurements over time or distance.

- Draw a line graph with x and y axes of appropriate scales.
- Plot the first set of figures, in the same way as you would on a normal line graph, and join.
- Plot the other set(s) of figures and join up the points.
- Once you have checked each pencil line, go over it in pen.
- Label each graph line clearly.
- Give the graph a title.
- You can plot different types of units on the same graph as long as they share the same x axis. For example, on a graph showing the number of farmworkers and farmworkers' wages, one y axis can represent number of farmworkers and another y axis can be drawn down the right-hand edge of the graph and an appropriate scale used for farmworkers' wages.

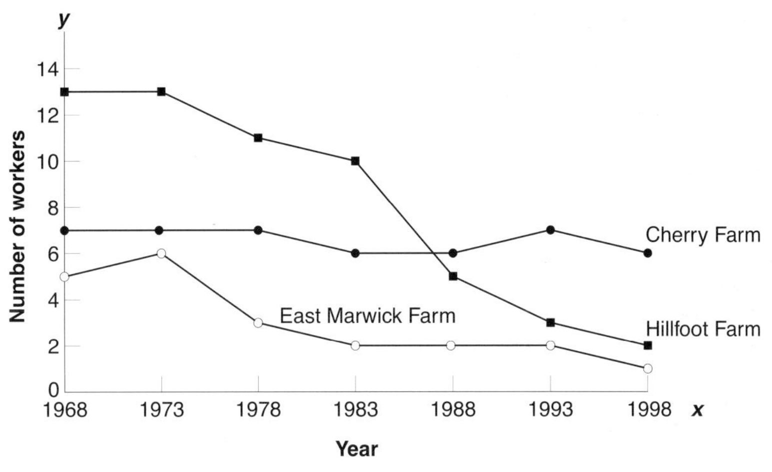

Figure 11.4 A multiple-line graph showing workers on three farms in Fife.

F Questions

Look at 11B.

F1 Which technique would you use to find out about (a) the land uses in an area of countryside and (b) a conflict between local people and the owners of a new factory?

Look at 11C.

F2 Write down two questions you would ask if you were interviewing a farmer about recent changes on his/her farm.

Look at 11D.

F3 (a) Copy the line graph in Figure 11.5.
(b) Complete the graph, using information from the table below.

Year	Number of farms in South Aberdeenshire
1941	37
1951	36
1961	34
1971	31
1981	29
1991	26

Look at Figures 11.6 and 11.7.

F4 Which table of information – Figure 11.6 or 11.7 – would be better shown on a line graph?

Figure 11.6 Land uses on Radwell farm

Land uses	Area (ha)
barley	10
grass	60
turnips	20
oats	20

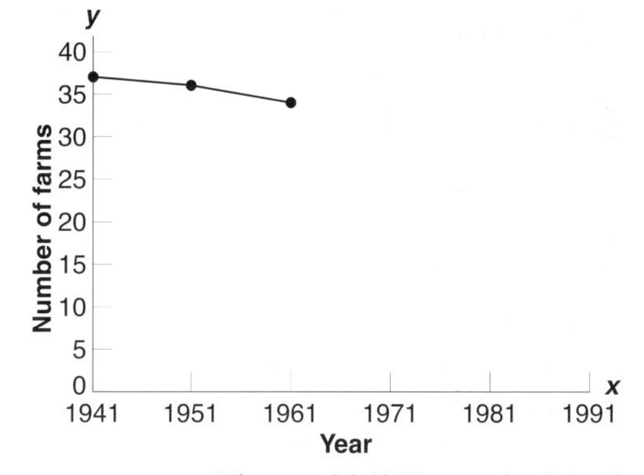

Figure 11.5 Farms in South Aberdeenshire.

Figure 11.7 Field size on Newland Farm

Field size (ha)	Distance from farmhouse (km)
1.0	0
1.0	0.5
2.4	1.0
3.2	1.5
4.3	2.0
4.9	2.5

Figure 11.8 Soil and height on Balmain's Farm

Height (metres)	Soil (pH)
100	7.2
200	6.4
250	5.4
200	6.7
100	6.3
150	6.5

G Questions

Look at 11B.

G1 Which technique would you use to gather information on (a) a conflict between a new factory and the local people and (b) changes in an area of countryside over the last 20 years? Give a reason for each answer.

Look at 11C.

G2 (a) When interviewing someone, why is it helpful to have the questions already written down?
(b) Write down the questions you would ask if you were interviewing a farmer about his/her farm inputs.

Look at 11D.

G3 Draw a line graph to show the information from the table below.

Average milk yield for cows in Scotland

Year	Milk yield (litres)
1944	2400
1954	3200
1964	3500
1974	3500
1984	5000
1994	5300

Look at Figures 11.6 and 11.7.

G4 Which table of information – Figure 11.6 or 11.7 – would be better shown on a line graph? Give a reason for your answer.

Look at 11B.

C1 Which techniques would you use to gather information on (a) the inputs and outputs of a farm and (b) the distribution of woodland in an area? Justify your choice of techniques.

Look at 11C.

C2 (a) Describe how you would prepare for an interview with a farmer.
(b) If you were investigating recent changes in a village, what questions would you ask a local resident?

Changes in Scottish agriculture 1944–94

Year	Tractors	Workers	Horses
1944	19 000	120 000	95 000
1954	42 000	90 000	30 000
1964	60 000	60 000	4000
1974	60 000	40 000	800
1984	59 000	30 000	500
1994	58 000	25 000	100

Look at 11E.

C3 Draw a multiple-line graph to show the information from the table above.

Look at Figures 11.6, 11.7 and 11.8.

C4 Which table of information – Figure 11.6, 11.7 or 11.8 – would be best shown on a line graph? Give a reason for your answer.

UNIT 12

Arable Farming

Core Text

12A FARMING TYPES

Farming, or **agriculture**, is the growing of crops and the raising of animals. In the UK, many different crops are grown and a variety of animals are raised, but all farms can be divided into three types:

1. **arable farms** on which most of the land is used for growing crops
2. **livestock farms** on which most of the land is used for animals
3. **mixed farms** on which the land is used for both crops and animals.

12B A FARM SYSTEM

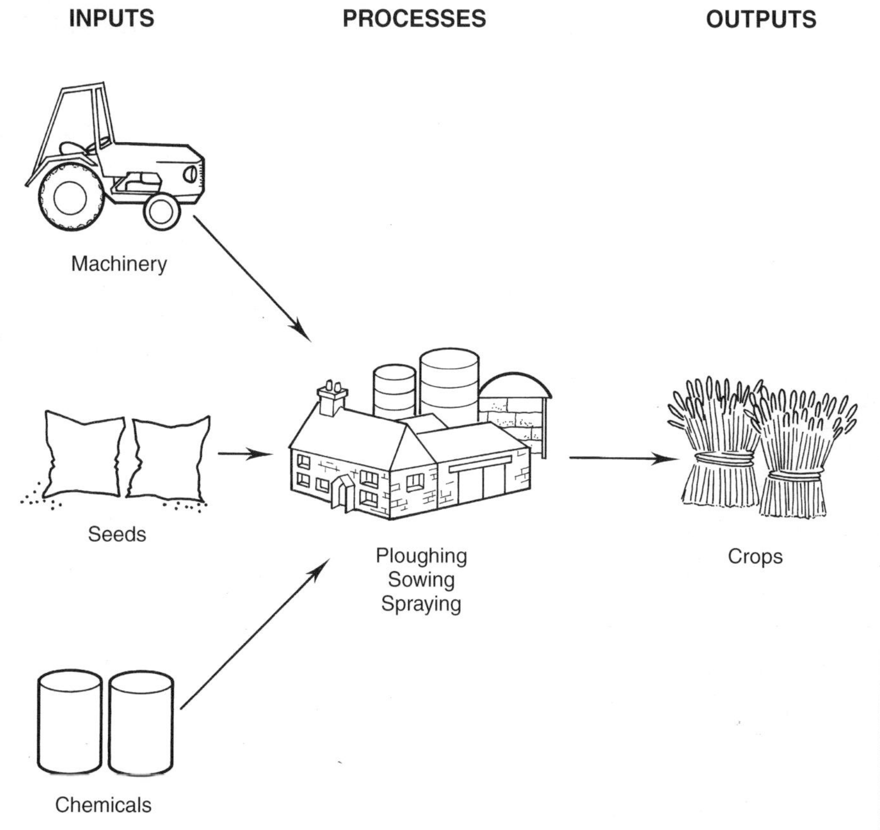

Figure 12.1 The farm system of an arable farm.

The products that a farm produces (such as beef, wheat or wool) are called its **outputs**. All the things needed to produce these outputs (such as seeds, crops and animal feed) are called **inputs**. Many jobs have to be done on a farm, for example, ploughing and harvesting, and these are called **processes**. A farm system is made up of inputs, processes and outputs. Figure 12.1 shows the inputs, processes and outputs of an arable farm.

12C FARM INPUTS

An arable farm needs many inputs for the crops to grow well. Some are natural or **physical** inputs; others are man-made or **human** inputs. Some of a farm's inputs are free, for example, rain or sunshine, but the farmer has to pay for most of the inputs.

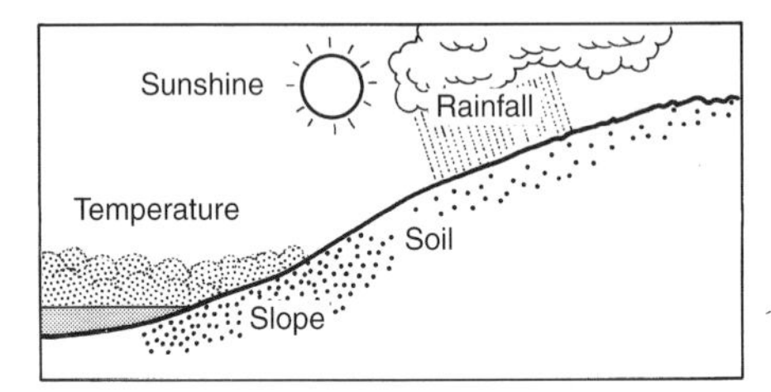

Figure 12.2 Physical and human farm inputs.

12D FARM OUTPUTS

In the UK, arable farmers grow most of their crops to sell. These are called **cash crops**. They may keep some animals and use some of their crops to feed them. These are called **fodder crops**. In developing countries, most farmers grow crops to feed themselves and their families. These are called **subsistence crops**.

The most common types of crop are:

- **cereal** or **grain crops**, such as wheat, barley and oats
- **root crops**, such as potatoes, turnips and sugar beet
- **vegetables**, such as peas, beans and cabbages.

12E THE LOCATION OF ARABLE FARMING

Before deciding what to farm, a farmer needs to know how well crops will grow on his/her land. He/she needs to consider especially the following factors:

1 **the soil** – it should be fertile
2 **temperature** – it must be warm during the **growing season**
3 **rainfall** – there must be some rain, but not too much
4 **sunshine** – it must be sunny to ripen the crops
5 **the land** – it must be quite flat so the farmer can use machines
6 **the price** of the crops – the crops must fetch a high price if the farmer is to make a profit.

12F MARKET GARDENING

A **market garden** is a small farm where the farmer grows salad vegetables, fruit and flowers. The produce is sent straight to towns and cities to be sold. Because of this, the farmer has to consider different factors before deciding to grow fruit and vegetables.

1. **nearness to market** – the farm should be near a town so the produce can be sold fresh
2. **communications** – the farm needs to be near fast roads so the produce can be transported to the towns quickly
3. **slope** – the land should be quite flat for all the buildings needed
4. **temperature** – it must be warm for the crops to grow well
5. **rainfall** – the area needs to have plenty of rainfall in order to swell the fruit
6. **sunshine** – the area must be sunny to ripen the fruit
7. **soil** – the land must be fertile for the crops to grow well.

12G ARABLE FARMING IN SCOTLAND

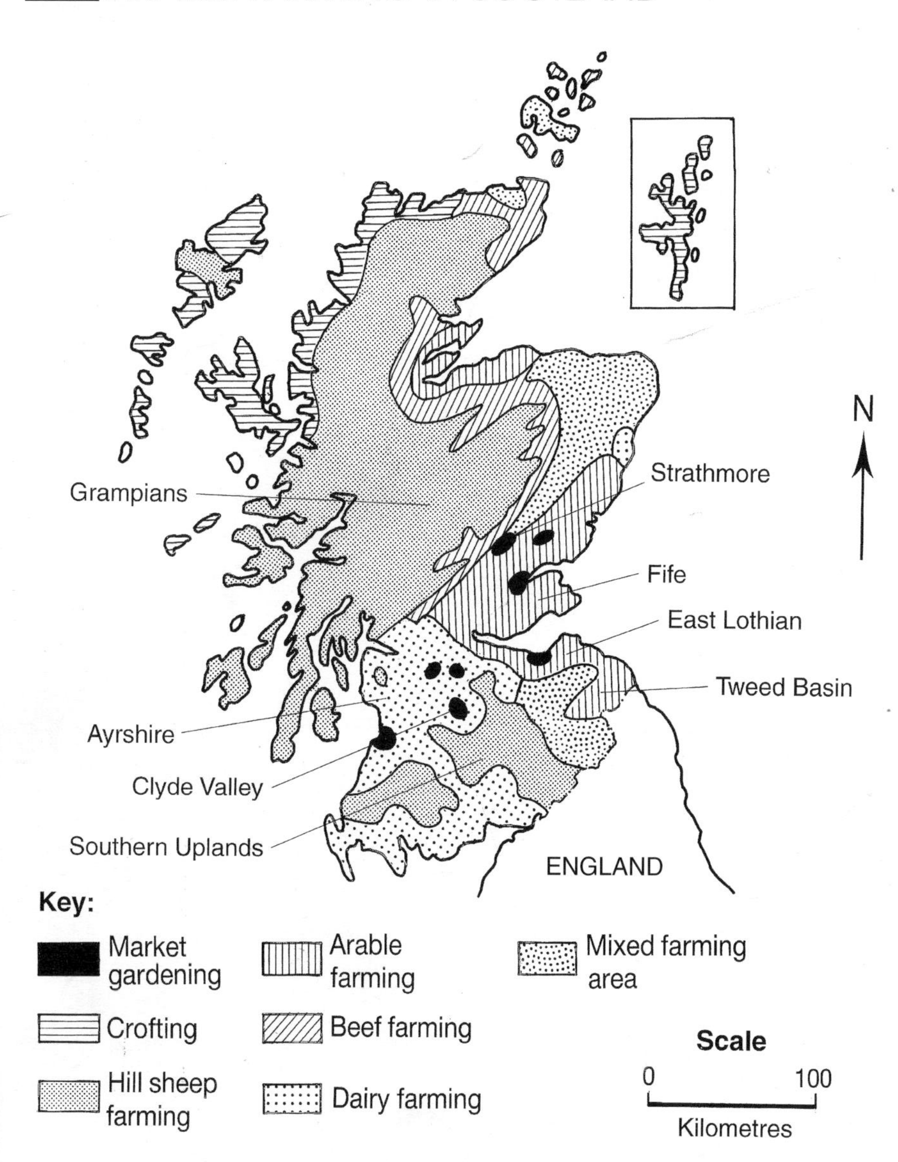

Figure 12.3 The farming regions of Scotland.

Most arable farms in Scotland are found:

1 **in lowlands** – where there is fertile soil, quite flat land and high temperatures
2 **in eastern Scotland** – where there is less rain and more sunshine.

The most important areas are Fife, East Lothian and the Tweed Basin.

Most market gardens in Scotland are found:

1 **in lowlands** – where there are high temperatures, fertile soil and quite flat land
2 **near cities** – so the product can be sold fresh.

The most important areas are the Clyde Valley and Strathmore.

12H INPUTS OF ARABLE FARMS

Figure 12.4

Average inputs per hectare of land (1997)

	Arable farm	Market garden
labour	£210	£1500
equipment	£200	£140
land	£130	£250
chemicals	£180	£400
seeds	£50	£10
packing, transport and others	£10	£2000

A market gardener spends more money on labour because he needs many workers to look after and harvest the many crops. The land is more expensive because it is usually near a large town. The market gardener uses lots of chemicals because he grows crops in each field or in greenhouses every year. He also spends more on packing and transport because he sends the produce to market on most days. An arable farmer spends more money on equipment because he needs expensive machinery such as combine harvesters.

12J LAND-USE PATTERNS ON A FARM

An arable farmer has to do a lot of work in the fruit and vegetable fields. So, in order to save time, these fields are located close to the farmhouse. Fields of cereal crops need less work, so they are located further from the farmhouse. If the farmer keeps sheep or beef cattle, these need very little attention and so will graze in fields furthest from the farmhouse. Dairy cows need to be milked twice daily, so they graze nearer the farm buildings (see Figure 12.5).

12K RECENT CHANGES

Arable farming has changed a lot in the last 20 years. There have been the following changes to farm inputs:

1 Farmers now spend more money on chemicals and farm machinery, but they employ fewer workers.

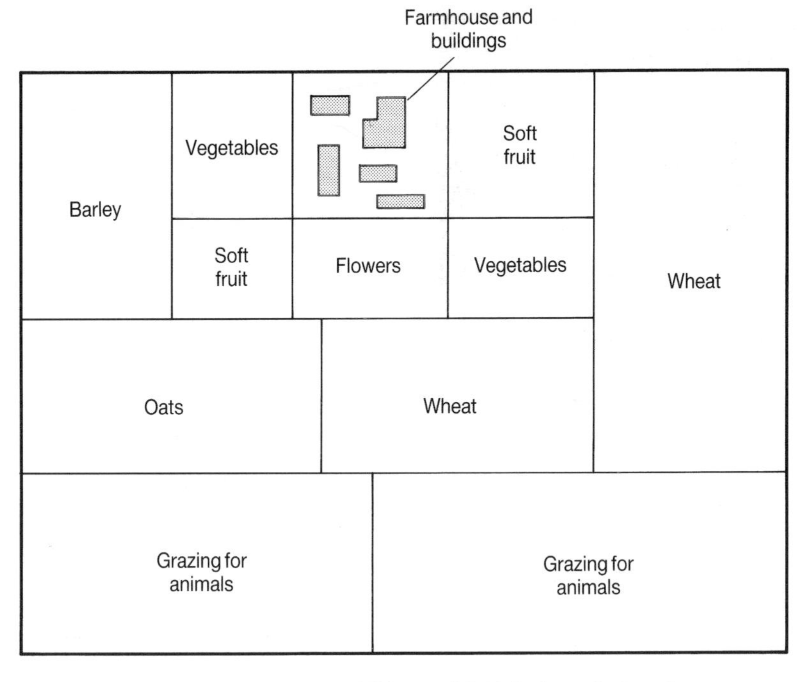

Figure 12.5 A farm's land-use pattern.

2 More machinery has led to larger farms and larger fields, as many hedges have been removed.
3 Since 1992, farmers have been given grants to improve the environment, for example, they are paid not to use chemicals on their farms (farms that do not use chemicals are called **organic farms**) and are paid to restore hedgerows.
4 Some market gardeners have changed to **pick your own (PYO) farming**. On these farms, customers pick their own fruit and vegetables from the fields. This is popular with customers because the produce costs less than it does in shops and is fresher. For the farmer, PYO means he/she has to employ fewer people. PYO farms have to be near towns and beside main roads to attract enough customers.

There have also been changes to farm outputs:

1 For many years the European Union (EU) has given farmers higher prices for some crops, such as cereals and peas. This has led to more of these crops being grown and not all of them being sold, creating a **surplus**.
2 Because too many of these crops were being grown, farmers are now paid not to grow crops but to leave their land fallow (unfarmed). This is called **set-aside land**.

12L OVERCOMING FARMING PROBLEMS

If farmers do not have ideal conditions for growing crops, they can try to improve the conditions so that crops will grow well. Some of the main ways they do this are shown in Figure 12.6.

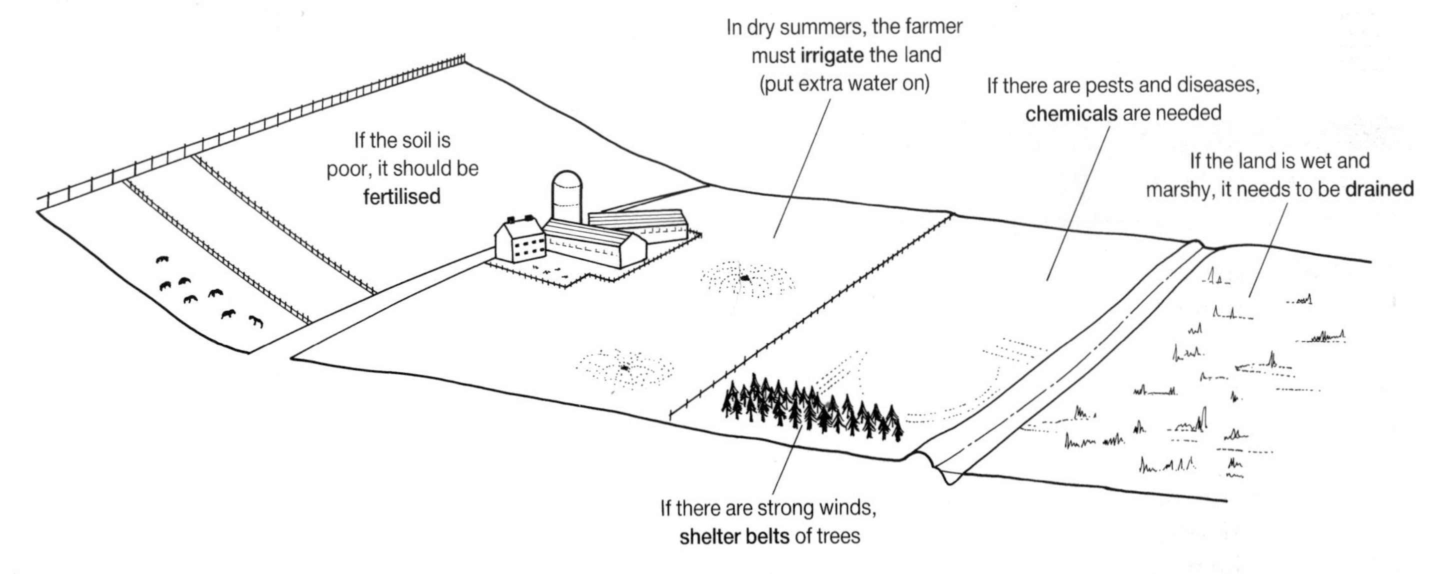

Figure 12.6 Methods for overcoming farm problems.

Core Questions

Look at 12A.

1 What is the difference between an arable and a livestock farm?

Look at 12B.

2 Which of the following words are (a) inputs, (b) processes and (c) outputs?
seeds, sowing, oats, ploughing, grain store, winter barley, harvesting

Look at 12F.

3 Which crops are grown on a market garden?

4 Why are market gardens found near large towns?

Look at 12G.

5 Give three reasons why eastern Scotland is important for arable farming.

Look at 12H.

6 On which type of farm is more money spent on inputs – an arable farm or a market garden?

Look at 12J.

7 Why are fruit and vegetables grown nearer to the farmhouse than wheat and barley?

Look at 12K.

8 What is meant by a crop surplus?

9 What is set-aside land?

Look at Figure 12.6.

10 Why do arable farmers (a) use shelter belts and (b) irrigate their land?

F Questions

CASE STUDY OF LINCOLNSHIRE

Look at Figure 12.7.

F1 Where are the main crop-growing areas in Lincolnshire?

Look at Figure 12.13.

F2 What were the four main crops grown in Lincolnshire in 1996?

Look at Figure 12.12.

F3 What are the main reasons why wheat is grown in the lowlands?

F4 What are the main reasons why peas are important on the Lincoln Marshes?

F5 What is the main reason why market gardening is so important in the Fens?

Look at Figure 12.13.

F6 Which crops were more important in 1996 than in 1971?

Look at Figure 12.14.

F7 In what ways has the European Union affected wheat farmers?

F8 Do you think the set-aside scheme is a good idea? Give reasons for your answer.

G Questions

CASE STUDY OF LINCOLNSHIRE

Look at Figure 12.8.

G1 Describe the distribution of (a) wheat and (b) sugar beet in Lincolnshire.

Look at Figure 12.12.

G2 What are the main reasons why wheat grows well here?

G3 Describe one advantage and one disadvantage of market gardening in the Fens.

G4 Why do you think oil-seed rape is an important crop in Lincolnshire?

Look at Figures 12.8 and 12.12.

G5 Do you think the Vale of Trent is suitable for pea-growing? Give reasons for your answer.

Look at Figure 12.13.

G6 Describe the main changes in farming land use in Lincolnshire between 1971 and 1996.

Look at Figure 12.14.

G7 Describe the main reasons for these changes.

G8 Describe one advantage and one disadvantage of the set-aside scheme.

CASE STUDY OF LINCOLNSHIRE

Figure 12.7

The Physical Landscape

Lincolnshire is a county in eastern England. As Figure 12.8 shows, the landscape is a mixture of dry, low hills and damp, clay vales. Crop-growing is especially important in the lowlands. The soils range from deep, fertile clays on the lowlands to poor, thin soils on the hills. Lincolnshire has warm summers of 16 °C, and winters of 4 °C and it is one of the driest and sunniest areas in the UK, with only 600 mm of rain per year.

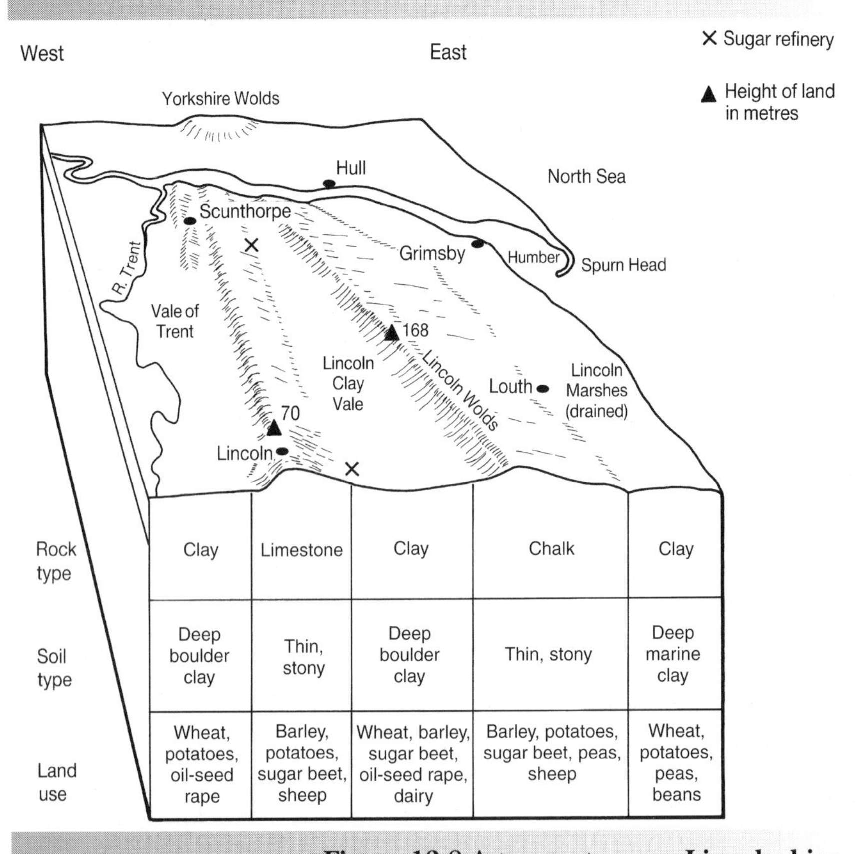

Rock type	Clay	Limestone	Clay	Chalk	Clay
Soil type	Deep boulder clay	Thin, stony	Deep boulder clay	Thin, stony	Deep marine clay
Land use	Wheat, potatoes, oil-seed rape	Barley, potatoes, sugar beet, sheep	Wheat, barley, sugar beet, oil-seed rape, dairy	Barley, potatoes, sugar beet, peas, sheep	Wheat, potatoes, peas, beans

Figure 12.8 A transect across Lincolnshire.

Figure 12.9 Farmland in Lincolnshire.

Figure 12.10

Improvements to the Landscape

Although Lincolnshire is well-suited to growing crops, people have made it even better. They have even reclaimed some land from the sea in the south of the county. It was drained by means of ditches and channels over 300 years ago. But, as they did so, the soil shrank and the height of the land fell by up to 4 m. So, windmills and, later, electric pumps were needed to pump the water from the fields onto the higher ditches. The dead-flat land is called the Fens and its soil is extremely fertile.

Other, smaller drainage schemes have also taken place in the Lincoln Marshes and the Clay Vale. Farmers have grown shelter belts of trees to protect the flattest areas from the wind, and many farms now have irrigation systems.

Figure 12.11 Farmland in the Fens.

Figure 12.12

Types of Farming

1 **Wheat** grows well in the lowlands of Lincolnshire because summer temperatures reach 16 °C. There is also plenty of sunshine, which is needed for the crop to ripen. Some rain falls in spring and early summer when it is needed for growth. The land is flat, which allows large machines to be used. The clay soils are ideal for wheat, as long as they are well-drained.
2 **Barley** can grow in cooler areas than wheat and where the soil is drier and sandier. This means it can be grown in the hills as well as the lowlands.
3 **Sugar beet** needs a deep, fertile soil. It needs warm, dry, sunny weather, especially at harvest time, and so it grows best in the lowlands. It is a heavy crop and this makes it expensive to transport. As a result, it is only grown near sugar-refineries.
4 **Peas** also need warm, dry, sunny summers and well-drained soils. Once harvested, they have to reach the processing works (a freezing or canning factory) within 40 minutes to retain their freshness. So, peas are grown near the processing works which, in Lincolnshire, are in the Grimsby area. Peas are an excellent **break crop**. This means that, when they are grown in a field after cereals, they make the soil fertile again so that it can be used for cereals the next year.
5 **Oil seed rape** does not need such warm temperatures as other crops but prefers heavy clay soils. It is a very useful break crop and can be grown on set-aside land, because it is an industrial crop rather than a food crop.
6 **Market gardening** is very important in the Fens. The chief crops are bulbs, flowers and soft fruit. Although the area is not very close to large towns or motorways, the climate is warm and sunny and the soil is extremely fertile. The Fens are world-famous for their bulbs.

Figure 12.13 Changes in farming in Lincolnshire 1971–96

% of total farmland occupied

	1971	1996
wheat	23%	39%
grassland	20%	11%
barley	27%	9%
set-aside	0%	9%
sugar beet	6%	7%
oil-seed rape	0%	6%
potatoes	5%	3%
beans	1%	2%
peas	1%	2%
other vegetables	7%	6%
others	10%	6%

Figure 12.14

Recent Changes in Farming

As Figure 12.13 shows, farmers in Lincolnshire now grow much more wheat, instead of barley, because for many years the European Union has guaranteed them high prices. Oil-seed rape is now grown, also because of the high price. Growing oil-seed rape in the UK means that we have to import fewer vegetable oils from overseas.

There is a lot of set-aside land now because farmers are paid over £250 per hectare not to grow crops on some of their land. As well as being paid, they have less to spend on labour, seeds, fertilisers and other chemicals and their machinery is used less. The land is also left fallow and wildlife increases. But, set-aside also means that useful farmland is being wasted and farmers are being paid to do nothing.

Extension Text

12M STANDARD WORK DAYS

The **standard work days (SWD)** are the number of days of work that a farm animal or crop needs in a year. For example, hay has an SWD of 2. This means that, in order for the hay to grow well and be harvested, two people must work for one day in that field or one person must work for two days.

Figure 12.15 below shows that some crops and animals need more time and attention than others. The farmer will try and locate the land uses with the greatest number of SWD nearest to his/her farmhouse.

Figure 12.15

	Standard work days per hectare		
hay	2	cauliflowers	50
cereals	5	peas	75
sugar beet	25	lettuces	75
potatoes	38	raspberries	200
cabbages	4		
	Standard work days per animal		
sheep	1	pigs	4
beef cattle	3	dairy cattle	10

12N LAND USES AROUND A CITY

Some land uses need to locate near a large town or city because their produce is perishable (for example, milk, flowers and vegetables) or because it is heavy and expensive to transport (for example, potatoes). Other types of farming can be carried out further away from towns. Figure 12.16 shows typical land uses around a city. It is based on the climate, relief, soils and communications being the same everywhere. In reality, these other factors will also vary and so produce a more complex pattern than that shown in Figure 12.16.

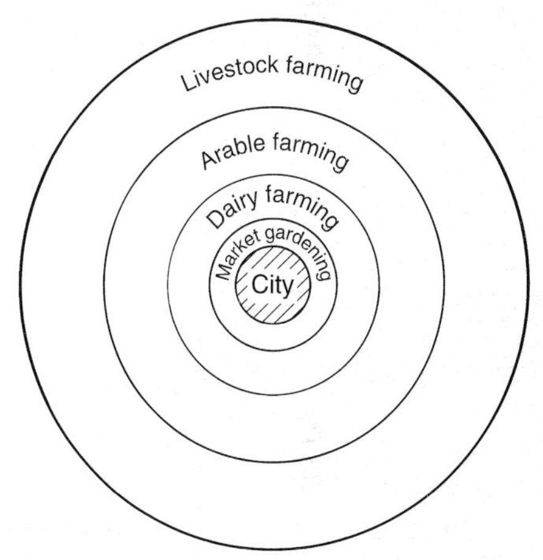

Figure 12.16 A model of land use around a city.

12P THE INFLUENCE OF THE EUROPEAN UNION

The European Union's **Common Agricultural Policy** offers farmers guaranteed prices in order that (a) they have a steadier income, (b) they can enjoy a higher standard of living and (c) the EU can be as self-sufficient as possible in farm produce. But, in recent years, this policy has led to huge surpluses (such as grain 'mountains' and milk 'lakes'), which cost millions of pounds to store. It is sometimes cheaper to let the crops rot in fields.

To reduce these surpluses, the EU began a set-aside scheme. Farmers who participate must take out of production some of their arable land (5 per cent in 1997) and, in return, receive a payment of over £250 per hectare.

12Q DECISION-MAKING IN FARMING

To make the greatest profit, a farmer must consider many factors before deciding what to farm. These are shown in the box below. The **natural factors** tell the farmer what types of farming the natural environment will permit. The **technological factors** show in what ways the natural environment can be improved to allow other types of farming to be practised. The **economic factors** show which of the possible types of farming is the most profitable for the farmer. This complex decision-making process is made even more difficult by the fact that many of these factors are constantly changing, for example, prices vary and technology improves (see Figure 12.17).

Figure 12.17

Natural factors	Technological factors	Economic factors
• temperature/length of growing season • total annual rainfall • amount of sunshine • soil quality • slope of land • pests and diseases	• availability and cost of irrigation • drainage • chemicals • new seeds • latest technology	• price of products • nearness to market • Government aid • EU aid

E Questions

Read the Extension Text.

E1 Explain why the set-aside scheme was introduced.

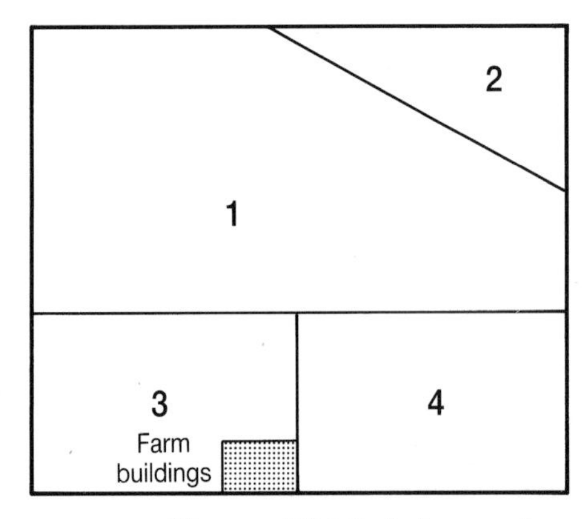

Figure 12.18 A farm plan.

Look at the farm plan in Figure 12.18.

E2 The farmer wishes to use one field each for barley, dairy cattle, potatoes and sheep. According to standard work days (SWD), which field should be used for each land use?

E3 (a) Explain the land-use pattern in Figure 12.16.
(b) In what ways is the diagram simplified?

C Questions

CASE STUDY OF LINCOLNSHIRE

Look at Figure 12.12.

C1 Describe the physical conditions that make wheat-growing possible in Lincolnshire.

C2 In what ways do human factors affect the distribution of peas and sugar beet?

C3 What are the main reasons why oil-seed rape is important in the Lincoln Clay Vale?

Look at Figure 12.10.

C4 In what ways do you think improvements to the landscape have affected farming here?

Look at Figures 12.13 and 12.14.

C5 In what ways has the European Union affected farmers in Lincolnshire in recent years?

C6 What different points of view do you think farmers in Lincolnshire have towards the set-aside scheme?

UNIT 13

Livestock and Mixed Farming

Core Text

13A DAIRY FARMING

Dairy farming (dairying) is a type of livestock farming in which cows are reared for their milk. The most common breeds used for dairying are Friesians, Ayrshires, Jerseys and Guernseys.

Before deciding to take up dairying, a farmer has to consider the following factors:

1. **temperature** – it must be warm for the grass to grow well, so the cows produce a lot of milk
2. **rainfall** – there must be sufficient rainfall for the grass to grow well
3. **soil** – the soil has to be quite fertile to produce good grass
4. **slope** – the land should be quite flat so that the dairy cows can graze
5. **nearness to market** – the farm should be near a town so the milk can be delivered fresh to the dairy.

Most dairy farms in Scotland are found in:

1. **lowland areas**, where there are higher temperatures, fertile soils and quite flat land
2. **in western Scotland** where there is more rainfall
3. **near towns**.

The most important dairying area is Ayrshire (see Figure 12.3, page 99).

13B HILL SHEEP FARMING

A sheep farmer rears sheep for their meat and wool. Sheep are hardy animals and can live in cold, wet uplands and on steep slopes. They can also live in lowland areas, but here it is more profitable for the farmer to grow crops or keep cattle. Lambs, however, are often fattened on the richer grass which grows in the lowlands.

Before deciding to keep sheep, a farmer has to consider many factors. These are listed on the next page.

1 **temperature** – is it too cold or is the growing season too short to grow crops or lush grass?
2 **rainfall** – is it too wet for crops to grow well?
3 **slope** – is it too steep to use the machines needed on a crop farm?
4 **soil** – is the soil too poor to grow crops?

Sheep farming areas in Scotland are mostly found in uplands, where the land is unsuitable for growing crops and keeping other animals. The most important areas are the Southern Uplands and the lower slopes of the Grampians (see Figure 12.3). The highest mountains in Scotland are unsuitable for any type of farming.

13C MIXED FARMING

Mixed farms are farms that produce both crops and animals. They are the most common types of farm in Britain and are found in areas where some of the farmer's land is good enough for crop growing but some is only suitable for livestock. In particular, mixed farming is found in areas that are not rainy enough for dairying nor sunny enough for arable farming and not poor enough for hill sheep (see Figure 13.1).

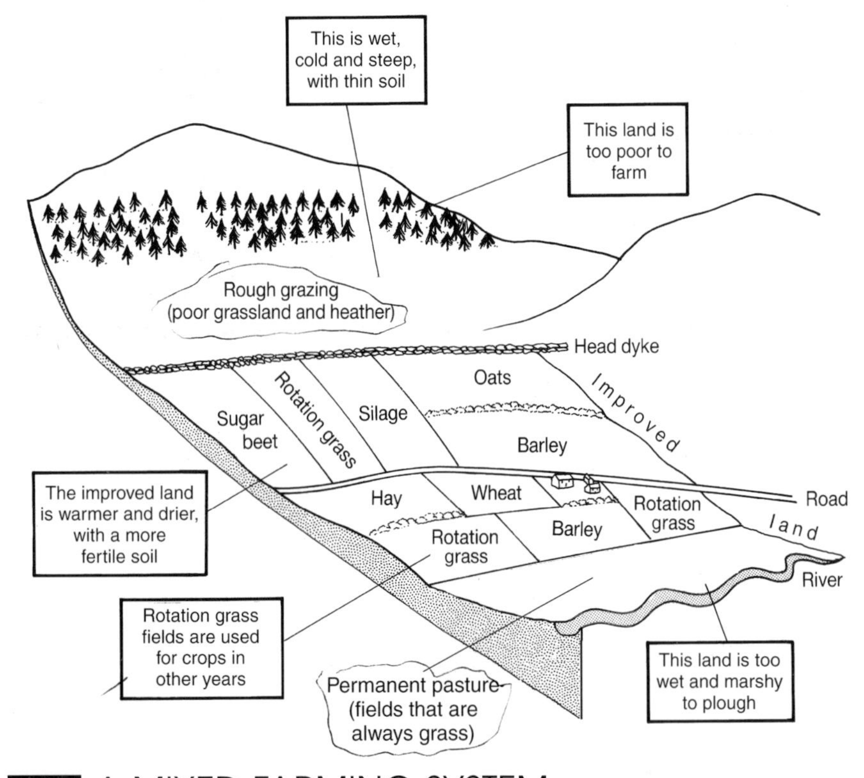

Figure 13.1 Land-use on a valley side.

13D A MIXED FARMING SYSTEM

A mixed farm has many outputs, which is safer for the farmer. If the price of crops is low, he/she may still get a high price for the animals, and vice versa.

A mixed farm has many inputs, most of which have to be bought. But mixed farmers are able to reduce costs by:

1 using animal manure as a fertiliser, instead of buying artificial fertilisers

2 growing fodder crops for the animals, instead of buying feedstuffs. Grass may also be grown as fodder, either for hay (dried grass) or silage (grass kept moist)
3 practising **crop rotation**. Growing some crops, such as cereals, makes the soil less fertile. Growing other crops, such as grass, peas and root crops, makes the soil more fertile. So, if a farmer changes the crops in each field every year or every few years, it helps to keep the soil fertile and so less money has to be spent on fertilisers. Figure 13.3 shows how one field on a farm might be used over six years.

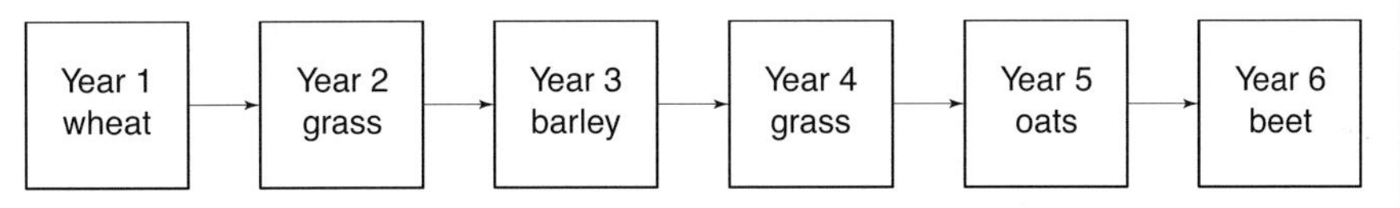

Figure 13.3 A six-year crop rotation system.

13E INTENSIVE AND EXTENSIVE FARMING

As Figure 13.4 shows, a dairy farmer spends large sums of money on each area of land. This is called **intensive farming**. Arable farming is another example of intensive farming. A hill-sheep farmer only spends a little money on each area of land. This is called **extensive farming**.

FARM INPUTS TO ONE HECTARE OF LAND (1996 average)

	Dairy farm		Sheep farm	
Labour	£410	many jobs to do such as milking and ploughing	£150	few jobs for much of the year
Machinery	£290	needs expensive machines like milking machines and harvesters	£100	few machines on steep land
Land	£220	expensive, good quality land	£80	cheap, poor quality land
Feedstuffs	£680	cattle kept indoors in winter and fed	£100	sheep graze outdoors all year
Fertiliser	£220	essential for grass to grow well	£60	most land not worth improving
Total	£1820		£490	

Figure 13.4 Inputs of dairy farming and sheep farming.

13F RECENT CHANGES

Since 1984, the European Union has set a limit on the amount of milk that British farmers can produce and sell. This limit is called a **quota**. Each farmer has a quota of milk that he/she is allowed to sell. If a farmer wants to have more cows and sell more milk, he/she must buy another farmer's quota.

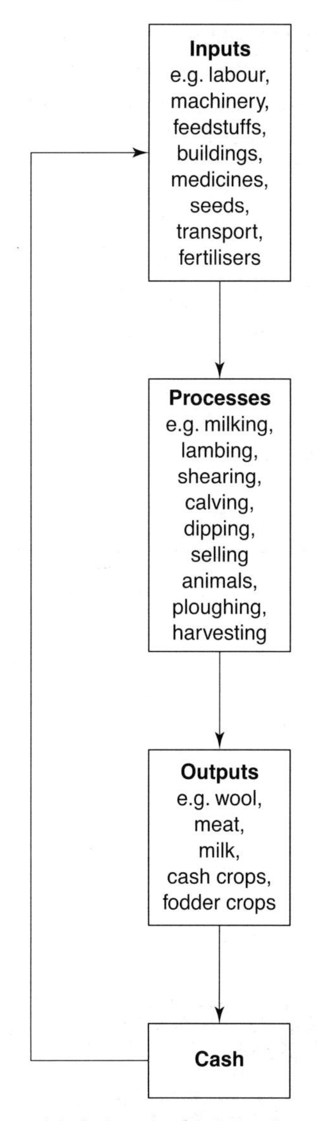

Figure 13.2 A mixed farming system.

Quotas were started because European farmers were producing too much milk and butter. Quotas have led to fewer dairy farms and dairy cows in Britain.

Extra money or **subsidies** are now paid to hill farmers for every cow or sheep they own. This has been done to give hill farmers a higher standard of living.

Some farmers try to increase their profits by welcoming tourists. They do this by (a) having 'leisure farms' which tourists can visit, (b) using their fields for camp and caravan sites, (c) providing bed and breakfast accommodation, and (d) allowing their land to be used for recreation, for example, motor bike scrambling and paintballing.

Core Questions

Look at 13A.

1 Why does a dairy farm need to be in an area with high temperatures?

2 Why are many dairy farms located near towns?

3 Why are many dairy farms located in western Scotland?

Look at 13B.

4 Give three reasons why sheep farming is found in upland areas.

Look at Figure 13.1.

5 What is meant by (a) permanent pasture, (b) rough grazing, and (c) rotation grass?

Look at 13D.

6 What is the difference between hay and silage?

7 What is crop rotation?

Look at 13E and Figure 13.5.

8 Which is more intensive – farm A or farm B? Give a reason for your answer.

Figure 13.5

	Inputs (per hectare)	Outputs (per hectare)
Farm A	£500	£700
Farm B	£1000	£1100

Look at 13F.

9 What is a milk quota?

10 In what ways can tourists bring farmers money?

F Questions

CASE STUDY OF HODDOMTOWN FARM

Look at Figure 13.6.

F1 Where is Hoddomtown Farm located?

F2 Why does the farmer prefer mixed farming here?

Look at Figure 13.10.

F3 What are the two main land uses on the farm?

Look at Figure 13.11.

F4 Suggest why the farmer does not grow crops in the fields used as permanent pasture.

F5 What are the main reasons for keeping sheep on the farm?

F6 Do you think the farmer should keep dairy cattle? Give reasons for your answer.

Look at Figure 13.13.

F7 In what ways does the farmer keep the soil fertile?

Look at Figure 13.15.

F8 Is it a good idea for the farmer to have a caravan site on the farm? Give reasons for your answer.

G Questions

CASE STUDY OF HODDOMTOWN FARM

Look at Figure 13.8.

G1 Describe the physical landscape of Hoddomtown Farm.

Look at Figure 13.11.

G2 Suggest why crops are not grown in all of the fields on the farm.

G3 What are the main reasons for keeping sheep?

G4 What are the advantages and disadvantages of keeping dairy cattle on the farm?

Look at Figures 13.8, 13.12 and 13.14.

G5 The farmer leaves one field as set-aside. If he had to leave another arable field as set-aside, which should he choose? Give reasons for your answer.

Look at Figure 13.15.

G6 If the farmer wanted to use his land differently, which of these would be best: (a) a small golf course, (b) a riding stable, (c) a caravan site? Give reasons for your answer.

CASE STUDY OF HODDOMTOWN FARM, DUMFRIESSHIRE

Figure 13.6

Introduction

Hoddomtown Farm is located beside a small tributary of the river Annan, 2 km south-west of the village of Ecclefechan in south-west Scotland. The main farm is 170 hectares in size, but the farmer also owns and rents land elsewhere around the village. It is a mixed farm, partly because some of the land is suitable for crop-growing and some is only suitable for livestock. The farmer also prefers to sell many products, in case the price of one of them should fall. Since the start of the BSE ('mad cow disease') crisis in the early 1990s, for example, the price of beef cattle has dropped by one-third.

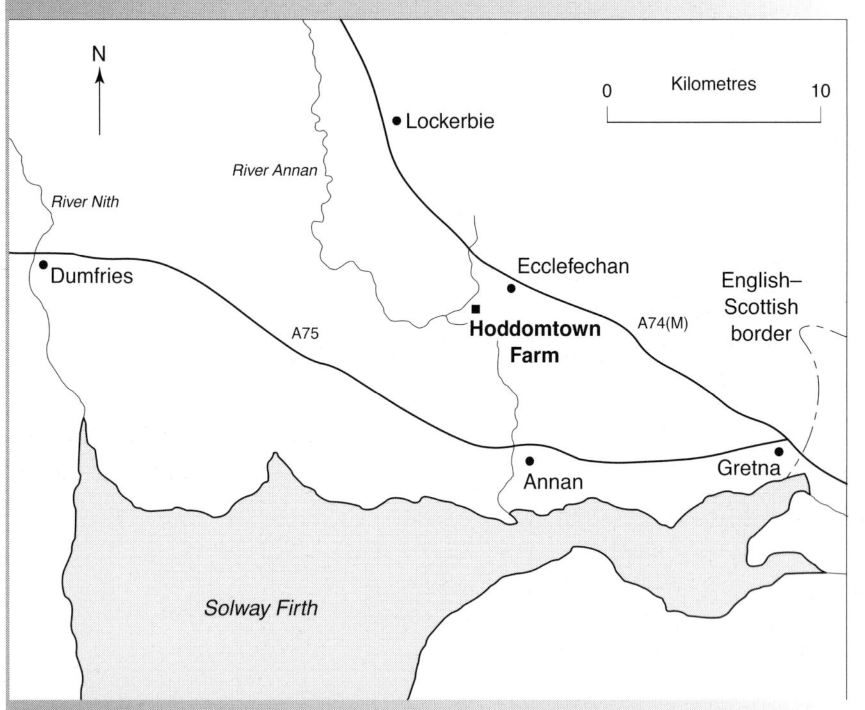

Figure 13.7 The location of Hoddomtown Farm.

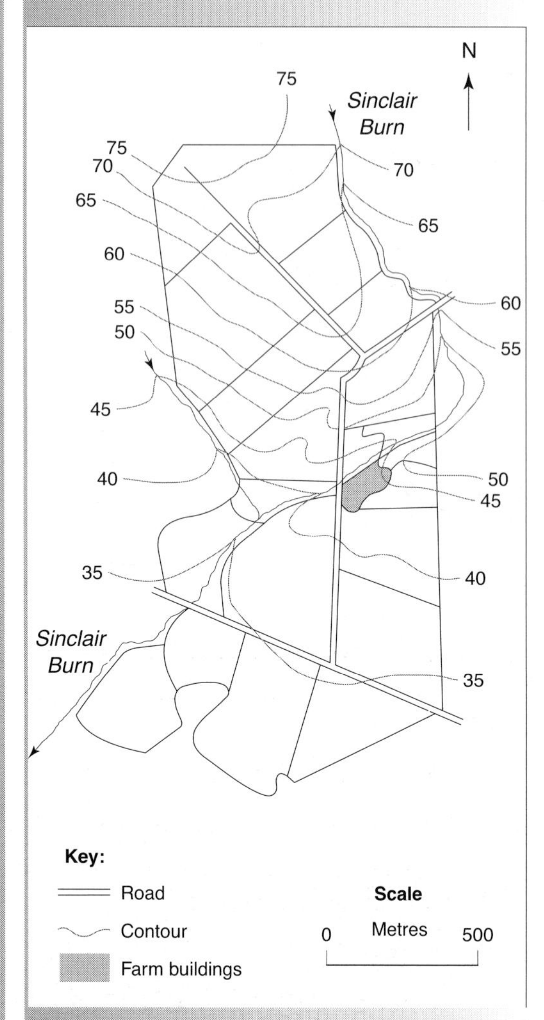

Figure 13.8 The relief of Hoddomtown Farm.

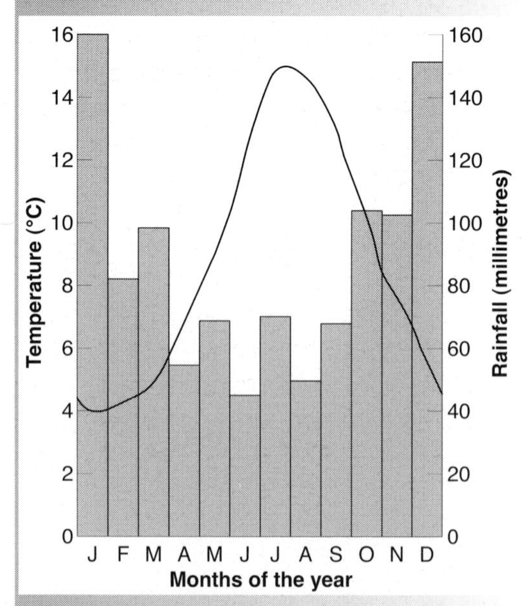

Figure 13.9 The climate of Hoddomtown Farm.

Figure 13.10

Land Uses

Outputs of Hoddomtown Farm

barley	69 hectares
rotation grass	62 hectares
permanent pasture	26 hectares
set-aside	13 hectares
beef cattle	300
sheep	600

Figure 13.11

Reasons for Land Uses

- **Barley** needs the deepest soil to grow well and the combine harvesters need the flattest land. Some barley is kept as fodder for the cattle. Some is sold to breweries.
- **Rotation grass** is kept as grass for a few years and then ploughed up for crops. For this reason, it is also found in the flattest areas with the deepest soils. Some of the grass is used for grazing, some for silage and hay.
- **Permanent pasture** is land always kept as grass. These fields are a little too marshy to plough. They are also small and irregular-shaped, which would make it difficult to use large machines such as harvesters.
- **Beef cattle** are bought as bullocks from upland farms and fattened up on the best grass in the lowest area of the farm.
- **Sheep** are kept on the steepest slopes with the poorest soils because machinery cannot be used and so crops cannot be grown. Also in this poor soil the grass does not grow well enough for beef cattle to eat.
- **Dairy cattle** are not kept on Hoddomtown Farm. They would enjoy the rich grass here and produce much milk and there are small towns nearby where the milk could be sold. But they require a great deal of work and so a lot more wages would have to be paid and, before the farmer could begin, he would have to buy someone else's milk quota.

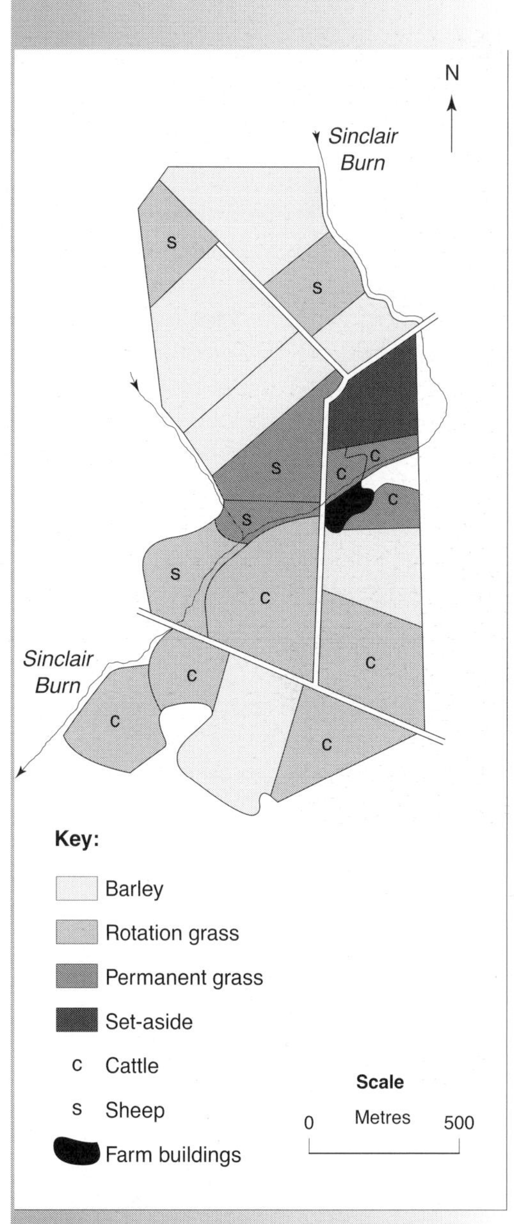

Figure 13.12 Land use at Hoddomtown Farm.

Figure 13.13

Improvements to Farm

- The farmer does rotate his crops in some of the fields, but keeps them fertile chiefly by adding lime to them.
- The farmer has installed drains in those fields with the flattest land where the water does not easily drain away – waterlogged soil does not contain enough air for crops to grow well.

Figure 13.14

Grants and Subsidies

1 **Set-aside** – the farmer is paid by the European Union not to grow crops on 5 per cent of his land. So he has set-aside the field with the poorest soil and drainage of all the arable fields.
2 **Subsidies** – the farmer is also given, by the European Union, two payments of over £80 for each of 90 cattle on the farm and they are given a payment each year for the sheep. The amount varies, but in 1996 was £13 for each sheep.

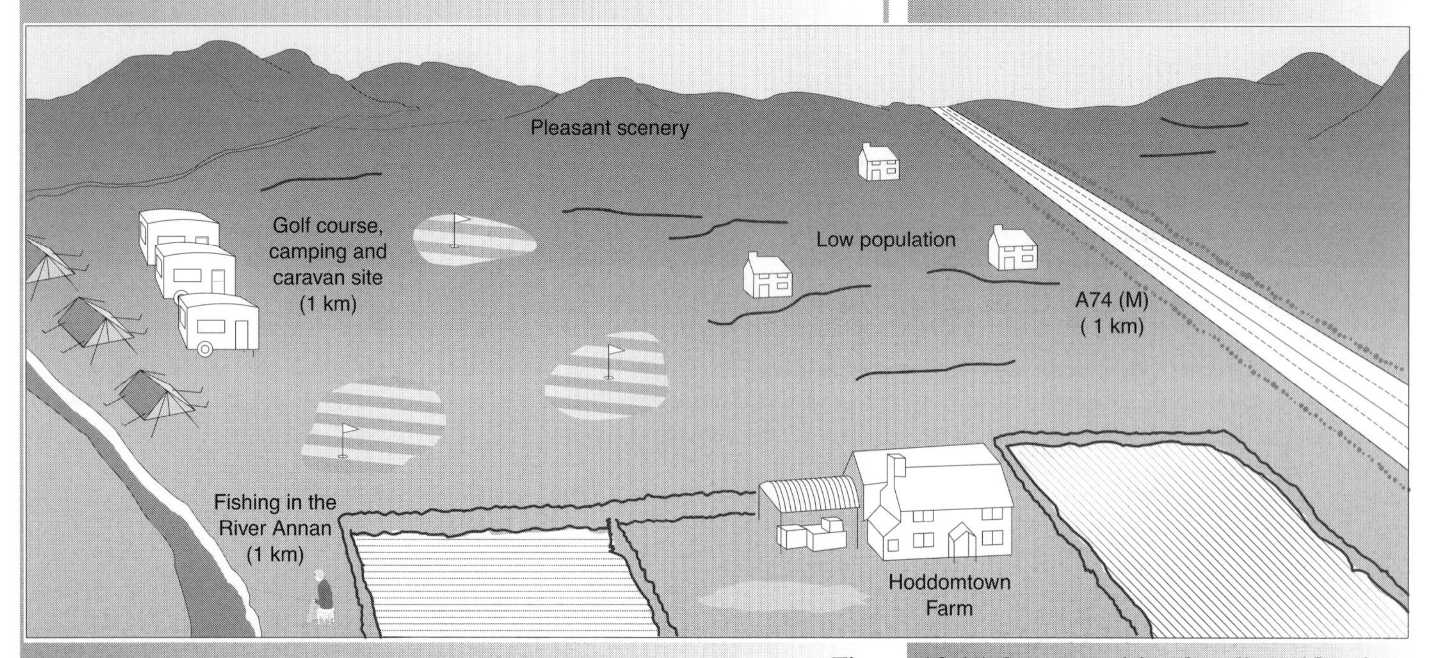

Figure 13.15 Opportunities for diversification.

Extension Text

13G CROFTING

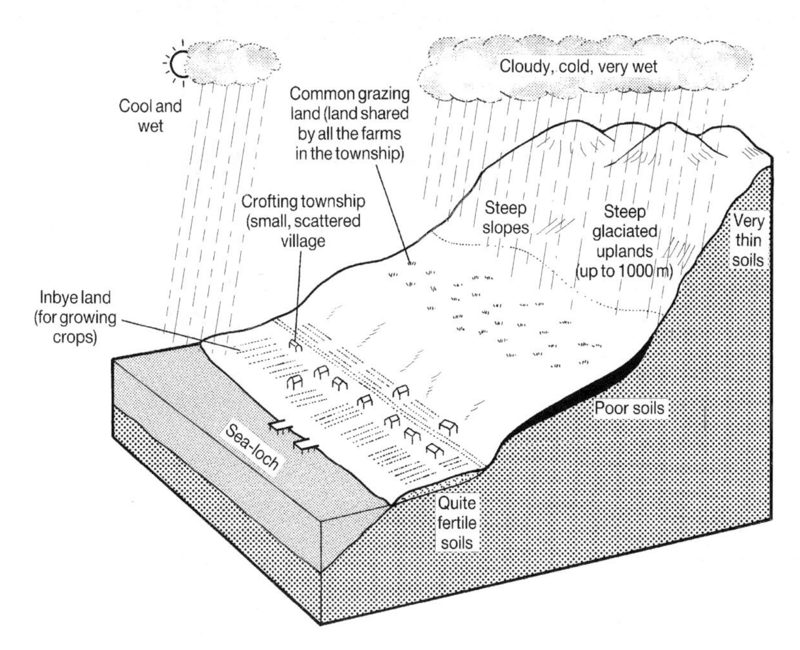

Figure 13.16 A typical crofting village.

Crofting is a type of farming found in north-west Scotland and the Scottish islands. Crofts are very small farms on which crops are grown on the lowest, flattest land while animals are grazed on the hillside, which is shared by all the crofters in the crofting village. As Figure 13.16 shows, conditions are so poor in these areas that it is difficult to make a living from crofting. So, most crofters also have other jobs, such as fishing, forestry or running bed and breakfast accommodation. The Crofters Commission helps crofters by giving grants and loans.

13H THE INFLUENCE OF THE EUROPEAN UNION

The European Union affects livestock farmers by:

1 imposing quotas, as described on page 111
2 in **less favoured areas** (poor farming areas), giving farmers grants for each head of livestock
3 giving grants to farmers who convert farmland into woodland
4 giving grants to farmers who diversify into other activities, such as golf courses, holiday cottages or pick-your-own farms.

E Questions

Read the Extension Text.

E1 What is crofting?
E2 Describe the physical inputs of a typical croft.
E3 What other occupations might crofters have?
E4 What are **less favoured areas**?
E5 What is meant by diversification?

C Questions

CASE STUDY OF HODDOMTOWN FARM

Look at Figures 13.6, 13.8 and 13.9.

C1 Describe the physical factors that affect farming on Hoddomtown Farm.
C2 Suggest reasons why the farm is a mixed farm.

Look at Figure 13.11.

C3 Describe the arguments for and against the farmer changing from beef cattle to dairy cattle.

Look at Figure 13.14.

C4 In what ways has the European Union affected land use on the farm?

Look at Figure 13.15.

C5 Do you think there are many opportunities for the farmer to diversify? Give reasons for your answer.

UNIT 14

Changes in the Countryside

Core Discussion 1

Figure 14.1 Changes to a lowland farm landscape in Europe between 1938 and 1998.

TASK 1: Divide into groups of three or four.
TASK 2: Look at the two pictures in Figure 14.1. They show the same lowland farm landscape in Europe in 1938 and 1998.
TASK 3: Elect a person in your group to write down your views.
TASK 4: Discuss the changes in the farm landscape since 1938.
TASK 5: Suggest reasons why the landscape has changed.
TASK 6: Present your views to the whole class.
TASK 7: Write a report on (a) recent changes in the European farm landscape and (b) the reasons for these changes.

Core Text

14A CHANGES IN POPULATION

There have been great changes in the countryside over the last 60 years. As well as the changes to the landscape, shown in Figure 14.1, there have also been changes to the population and to the settlements.

Many people have **emigrated** (moved away) from the countryside into towns and cities, and the number of people living in the countryside has declined. This is called **depopulation**. The main reasons for this are shown in Figure 14.2.

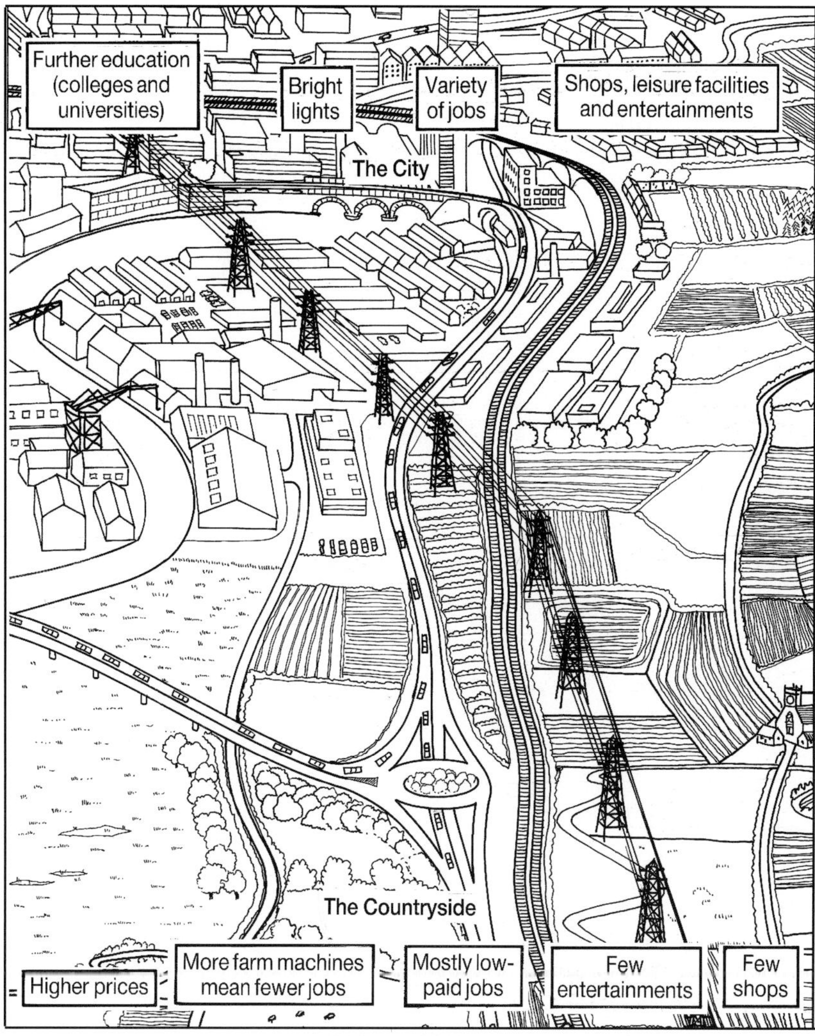

Figure 14.2 Reasons for migrating from the countryside to towns and cities.

14B CHANGES IN AGE GROUPS

Young people (aged 16–30) are the most likely to move away from the countryside. They do this to find a job, to study at a college or university, or to enjoy the entertainment found in cities. Older people who already have jobs and strong links in the area are much less likely to move away from the countryside. So, countryside areas have an increasing number of older people and fewer young people. This is called an **ageing population**.

14C CHANGES IN VILLAGES

As people move away from villages, there are not enough customers to keep shops, schools, pubs and other services open. So many of these services close. When they close, the village becomes even less attractive to live in and even more people leave.

14D SOLUTIONS TO POPULATION DECLINE

Several methods have been tried to improve conditions in the countryside so that people will not want to leave.

1. The EU's Common Agricultural Policy pays farmers higher prices for their crops and animals and gives subsidies to hill farmers. These should improve farmers' standard of living.
2. The government gives grants to companies that set up in the countryside and it also improves the roads in order to attract new companies. This should provide people with better paid jobs.
3. If the area can attract tourists, then there will be more jobs available (for example, in hotels, shops and restaurants) and fewer people will want to leave.
4. If local services are closing down, mobile services can be provided to visit every village (for example, mobile shops, libraries and banks).

14E MOVING BACK TO THE COUNTRYSIDE

Not all countryside areas have a declining population. Many people who work in a city prefer to live in the countryside and travel to work each day. Such people are called **commuters**. Many live in villages that have fast road and rail links to the city. These villages are called **dormitory villages** and have a growing population.

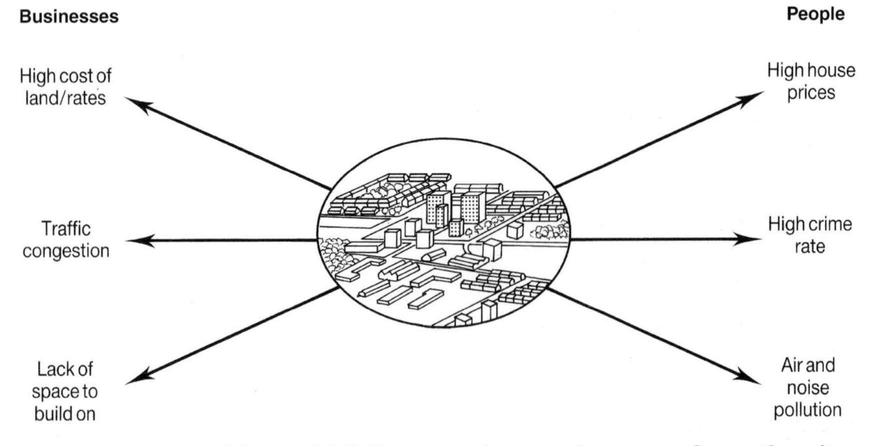

Figure 14.3 Reasons for moving away from the city.

Villages in more remote but attractive countryside areas (for example, on the coast, in uplands) are also increasing in population. Many people move there to retire and some people also buy houses in these villages as holiday homes or **second homes**. They can afford to pay high prices and so bring more money into the area. But local people cannot afford to pay these high prices and may be forced to leave the area. Also, second homes are not occupied for most of the year, so local shops, pubs, schools and bus services may have to close.

14F CONFLICTS IN THE COUNTRYSIDE

The countryside is not just used for farming. Increasingly, other land uses are to be found here and some create conflicts. Some of these are shown in Figure 14.4.

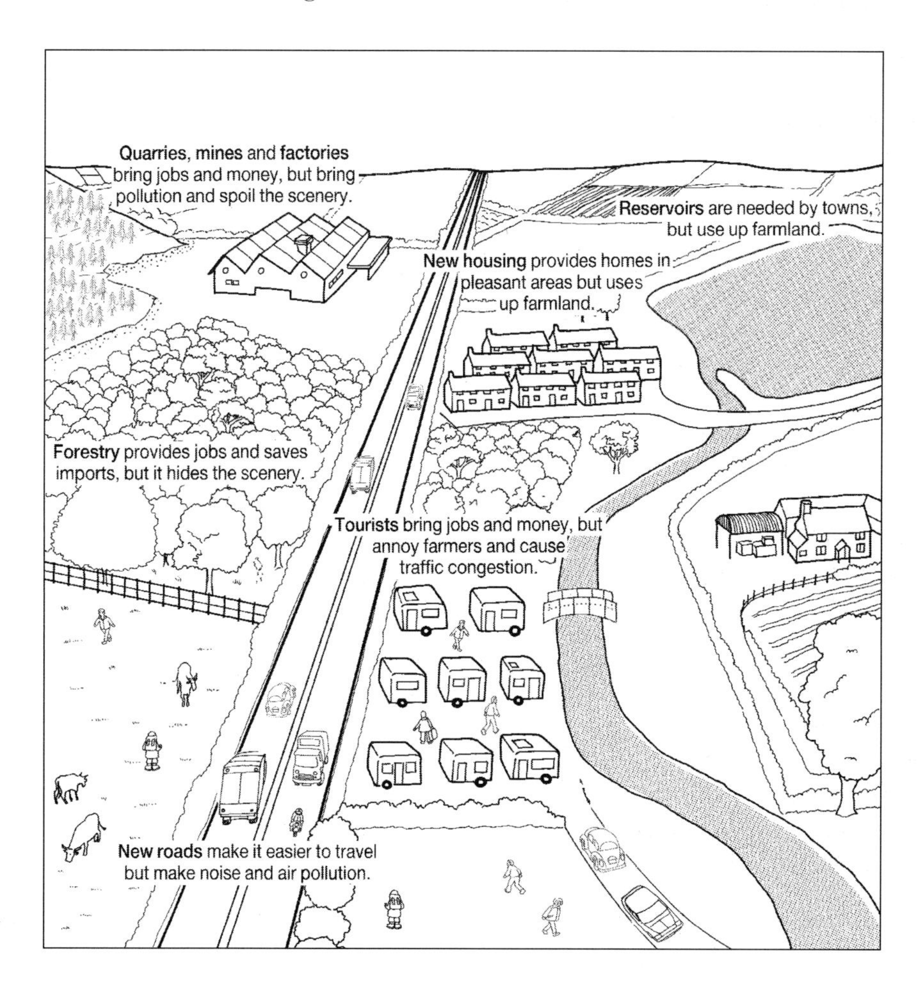

Figure 14.4 Common conflicts in the countryside.

14G CONSERVATION OF THE COUNTRYSIDE

As more countryside is being used for housing, roads and tourist facilities, steps are now being taken to **conserve** (protect) those areas of natural beauty that remain. The box below shows some of the main conservation areas in Britain. Within these areas, there are restrictions on the amount and type of development that can take place.

Some conservation areas are found in remoter, upland areas, for example, **National Parks**, while others, such as **Country Parks**, are found nearer to towns and cities. In these areas, facilities are provided for tourists. Green Belts are found at the edges of cities. Within these areas, it is difficult to obtain planning permission to build. Green Belts should prevent cities from spreading into the countryside.

Figure 14.5

Examples of conservation areas

National Parks
Country Parks
Nature Reserves
Bird reserves
Long-distance footpaths
National Scenic Areas
Green Belts

Core Questions

Look at Figure 14.2.

1 Name two problems in the countryside that persuade people to leave.

2 Name two attractions of cities which encourage people to move there.

Look at 14B.

3 Which age groups are most likely to move away from the countryside?

Look at 14C.

4 Why have many shops in villages closed in recent years?

Look at 14D.

5 In what way can tourism help to stop people leaving the countryside?

Look at Figure 14.3.

6 Give two reasons why many people now prefer not to live in cities.

Look at 14E.

7 What is a dormitory village?

Look at 14F.

8 Apart from farming, name three other important land uses in the countryside.

Look at 14G.

9 Why is it necessary to conserve areas of natural beauty?

10 Name two types of conservation area.

11 What is the purpose of a Green Belt?

Look at Figure 14.6.

12 Name the 12 National Parks in England and Wales.

Extension Questions

Look at 14E.

E1 What are the effects of having many second homes in a village?

E2 Where would you expect to find dormitory villages?

E3 Which of the four solutions in 14D will do most to reduce population decline in the countryside? Give reasons for your answer.

Look at 14G.

E4 What are the advantages and disadvantages of allowing factories to be built in a Green Belt area?

Look at Figure 14.6.

E5 Describe the distribution of National Parks.

E6 'All the people living in conurbations (large built-up areas) in England and Wales should have easy access to a National Park.' Do you think this aim has been achieved? Give reasons for your answer.

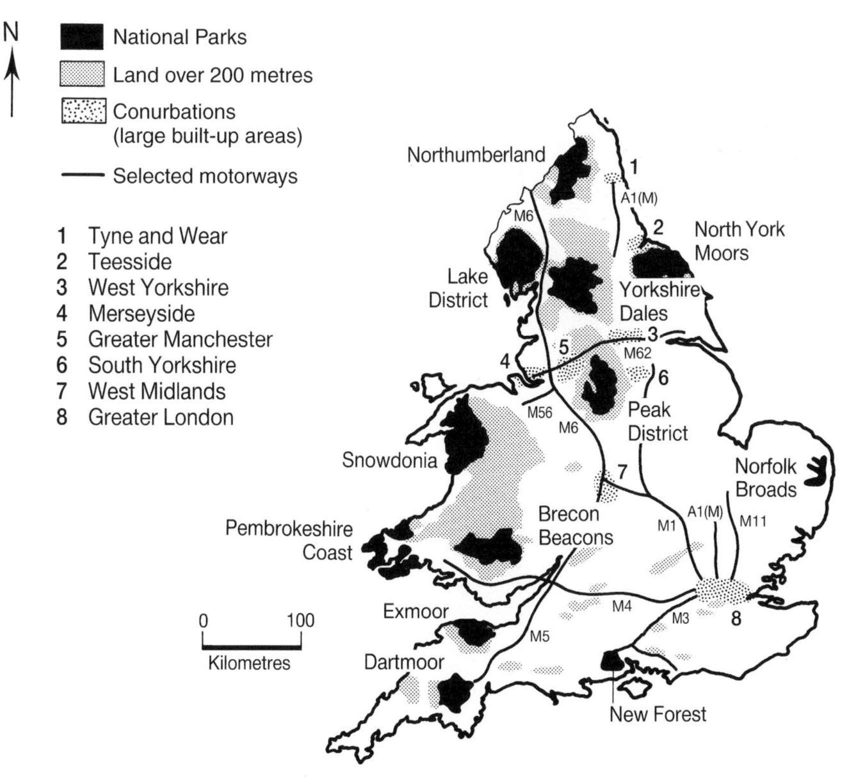

Figure 14.6 The National Parks of England and Wales.

Core Discussion 2

Braithwaite is a small village west of Keswick in the Lake District National Park. Like other villages, it has been through many changes. Some of these changes have been because it is located in a very popular and attractive area of Britain.

TASK 1: Look at Figures 14.8 and 14.9, which show some of the changes that have taken place in Braithwaite since 1951. Look also at the descriptions of Edie, Albert, Annie and Jim on page 125.

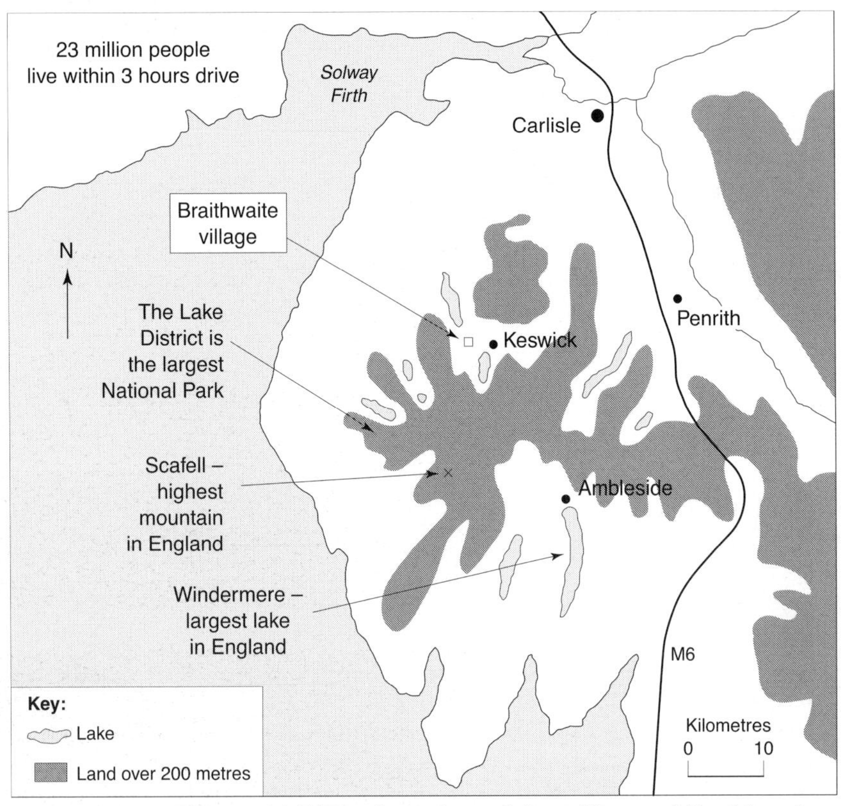

Figure 14.7 The location of the village of Braithwaite.

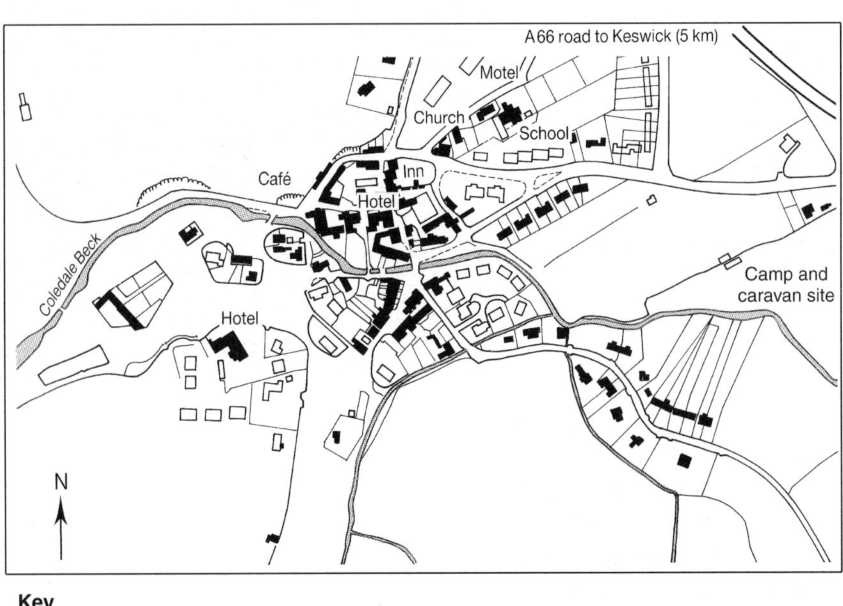

Figure 14.8 A map of Braithwaite.

TASK 2: In groups of four, write a discussion between Edie, Albert, Annie and Jim. Each person in the group should pretend to be one of the four characters. They should discuss how life in Braithwaite has changed since 1951 and whether it is better or worse now. Make sure each character talks about a different point (for example, how there were more shops in the 1950s, how there are more local jobs now). Each character can make as many statements as you wish.

Figure 14.9

	Braithwaite 1951	Braithwaite 1998
Population	650	580
Age group	young, middle-aged and old people	fewer young people and more old people
Services	2 general stores 1 pub 1 post office 1 primary school 1 cobbler	1 general store 3 pubs 1 post office 1 primary school 1 cafe
Jobs	most people worked in the town of Keswick	more local jobs in hotels and guest houses
Bus service	very frequent	fewer buses
Shop prices	similar to shops in Keswick	more expensive than the shops in Keswick

TASK 3: Once you have completed task 2, imagine that the characters have changed the topic of their conversation. Read the text below and work out how your character would feel about people buying second homes in Braithwaite. Then, write a discussion between the characters on the advantages and disadvantages of second homes and whether they should be allowed or not.

Figure 14.10

Second homes in Braithwaite

More and more houses in Braithwaite are now second homes. Some people are against this. They think it will destroy the character of the village and will not be in keeping with the aims of a National Park. They want houses in the village to be sold only to local people, while others think they should be sold to anyone.

If houses are sold to local people only, they would be much cheaper. If they are sold to anyone, they would probably become second homes for wealthy people who live elsewhere.

THE VILLAGE CHARACTERS

Edie

Edie is 58 years old and is a widow. She has lived in Braithwaite all her life and her mother and brother still live nearby. Edie cannot drive, so she uses the local services a lot. Her son is a qualified engineer who moved to Manchester in 1975 because there were no suitable jobs for him locally. Edie finds it difficult to talk to the 'newcomers', as she calls people who have recently moved to the village.

Annie

Annie is 63 years old and is divorced. She worked in the local grocery shop until it closed. Her daughter is a nurse who had to move away because she could not afford to buy or rent a house locally. An active conservationist, Annie thinks the village should stay the way it is and dislikes the village being overrun with tourists in summer.

Albert

Albert is 55 years old and married with no children. He was born in Braithwaite. He is a master joiner, whose main work is in Keswick, but he has had more local work recently from the owners of second homes. Albert owns a large house and his wife started offering 'bed and breakfast' accommodation 15 years ago, which is very profitable.

Jim

Jim is 40 years old and is married with one son. He has lived in Braithwaite since he was 6 years old and is worried that the primary school may close if no families with young children move in. He had steady work as a labourer until 10 years ago but has been mostly unemployed since, although he has done odd jobs in the village. Jim's wife recently started work as a cleaner in a local hotel. Most of his school friends moved away from the area a long time ago.

UNIT 15

Map Skills

Core Text

15A INTRODUCTION TO MAP SKILLS

Geographers study landscapes and try to work out why they look the way they do. A map is a view of a landscape as you would see it from directly above. Geographers make use of maps to find information about landscapes.

The **Ordnance Survey (OS)** is an organisation that produces many maps. Every Standard Grade Geography examination paper includes a map and it is nearly always an OS map.

For the Standard Grade examination, you need to be able to:

1 use grid references to locate places
2 work out height and slope
3 work out distance using a scale
4 work out directions
5 draw and interpret cross-sections and transects
6 identify landforms made by rivers and ice
7 identify land uses in towns and the countryside.

15B SCALE AND DISTANCE

A map is much smaller than the landscape it shows. The scale of the map tells us how much smaller it is. It tells us by how much real distances and sizes have been reduced. Scale can be shown on a map as a **linear scale** or as a **representative fraction**, such as 1 : 50 000.

A scale of 1 : 50 000 means that everything on the map is reduced to 1/50 000 of its real size. For every 1 cm on the map, there are 50 000 cm on the ground.

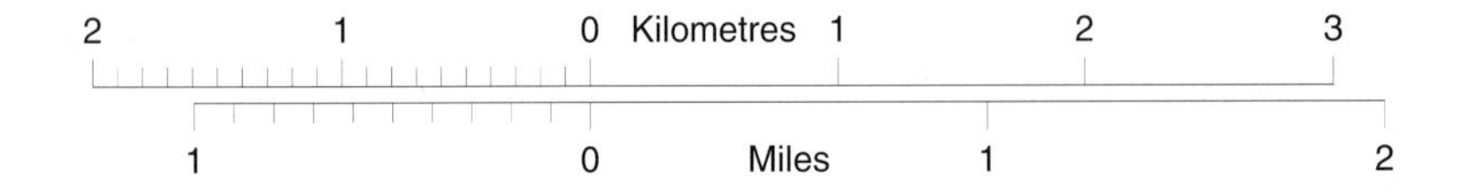

Figure 15.1 A linear scale representing 1 : 50 000.

To work out a distance between two places, you use the scale of the map. Measure the distance on the map and then either use the linear scale or multiply by the representative fraction to find the real distance. If a map is of a scale 1 : 50 000, any distance on the map has to be multiplied by 50 000 to find the real distance. On a 1 : 50 000 map, 2 cm represents 1 km.

15C DIRECTIONS

The vertical grid lines on an OS map point towards north (grid north). When giving directions, you should use the eight points of the compass, shown in Figure 15.2, and not words like top, bottom, left and right.

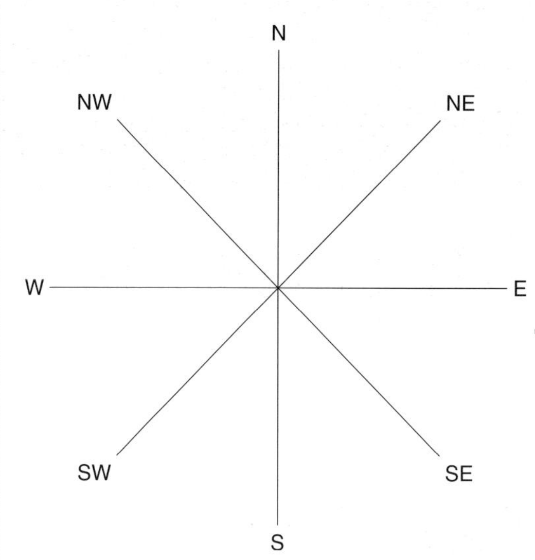

Figure 15.2 The eight points of the compass.

15D SYMBOLS

OS maps contain a great deal of information. There is not enough space to write it all on the map, so symbols are used. The symbols used on OS 1 : 50 000 maps are shown on the inside back cover of this book.

15E HEIGHT AND SLOPE

The height of the land is shown in two ways on OS maps.

1 **Spot heights**, which are black dots, have the height in metres next to them.
2 **Contour lines**, which are brown lines, join places with the same height. On 1 : 50 000 maps, contour lines are drawn 10 metres apart, as shown in Figure 15.3.

Contour lines also show the slope of the land. If the contour lines are close together, the slope is steep. If they are far apart, the slope is gentle (see Figure 15.3).

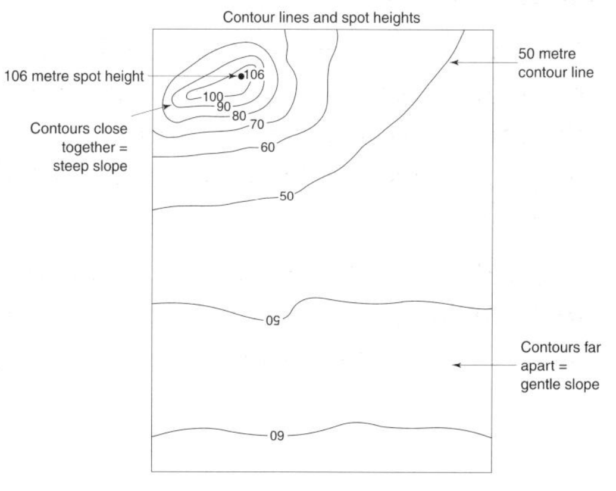

Figure 15.3 Contour lines and spot heights.

15F FOUR-FIGURE GRID REFERENCES

OS maps are divided into squares by blue grid lines running north to south and east to west. Places are located on OS maps using these grid lines.

A **four-figure grid reference** gives the location of a grid square. To work out a four-figure grid reference, for example, square A in Figure 15.4:

- note the number of the vertical grid line to the west (left) of square A (**45**)
- note the number of the horizontal grid line south of (below) square A (**86**).

The four-figure grid reference of square A = **4586**.

To find a four-figure grid reference, for example, square 4786:

- find the point where the 47 vertical grid line meets the 86 horizontal grid line
- square 4786 is to the north-east of this point (up and to the right).

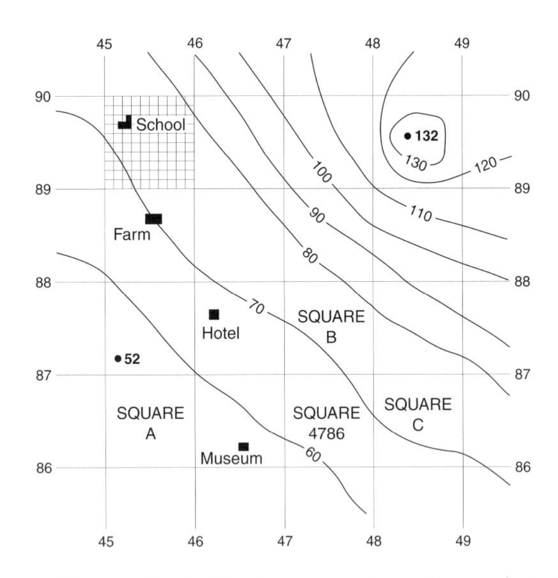

Figure 15.4 Working out four-figure grid references.

F Questions

Look at the OS map of Glasgow on the inside front cover of this book.

Look at square 5871.

F1 (a) Do you think the Roman Fort was easy to defend? Give reasons for your answer, using evidence from the map.
(b) Was it easy for the Romans living there to get water and wood? Give reasons for your answer, using evidence from the map.

F2 Do you think Glasgow is a tourist centre? Give reasons for your answer, using evidence from the map.

F3 Is square 5865 the CBD of Glasgow? Give reasons for your answer.

F4 Is square 5165 an old or new industrial area? Give reasons for your answer.

F5 Is the housing in square 5271 new? Give reasons for your answer.

F6 Describe the land uses in (a) square 5162 (b) square 5461.

Look at square 5770.

F7 (a) Is Blackhill Farm more likely to be an arable farm or a sheep farm? Give reasons for your answer.
(b) If the farmer sold the land, would it be a suitable place for an industrial estate? Give reasons for your answer.

F8 When the motorway in square 5462 was built, many people complained. Why do you think they complained?

G Questions

Look at the map of Glasgow on the inside front cover of this book.

G1 (a) Was the Roman Fort in square 5871 a good defensive site? Give reasons for your answer.
(b) Apart from defence, was it a suitable place for people to live long ago? Give reasons for your answer.

G2 What map evidence is there to show that Glasgow is an industrial centre?

G3 Is square 5965 the CBD of Glasgow? Give reasons for your answer.

G4 Which square has newer housing – square 5271 or 5862? Give reasons for your answer.

G5 Describe the land-use pattern in square 5971.

G6 What type of farming do you think takes place at Blackhill Farm (square 5770)? Give reasons for your answer.

G7 Port Dundas, in square 5966, has an industrial estate. Is this a suitable location for an industrial estate? Give reasons for your answer.

G8 When the M77 was built in squares 5462 and 5361, it caused much conflict. Describe, in detail, one argument for and one argument against building this motorway.

Extension Text

15G SIX-FIGURE GRID REFERENCES

Four-figure grid references locate grid squares. To locate exact points, **six-figure grid references** are needed.

To work out a six-figure grid reference, for example, for the school in Figure 15.3, imagine that square 4589 is divided into 100 smaller squares. The school is **2** small squares east of the **45** easting and **7** small squares north of the **89** northing. So, the six-figure grid reference of the school is **452897**.

15H DRAWING A CROSS-SECTION

A **cross-section** is a side view of the landscape. It shows the exact shape of the physical landscape. To draw a cross-section:

- Place a strip of paper over the line of your section on a map, and mark where each contour crosses the edge of the paper.
- Write down the height of each contour next to its mark and also write down the names of other features, such as rivers, that you have marked.
- Draw a graph with a horizontal (x) axis the same length as the line of your section.
- Choose a suitable scale and draw a vertical (y) axis for the graph.
- Place the paper below the graph and draw pencil lines from each contour mark to the correct height on the graph (see Figure 15.5).
- Join the points at the top of each line to produce the cross-section and rub out the pencil lines.
- Write the names of the other features on your section.
- Underneath the two axes, write the grid reference of your starting point and finishing point.
- Give the cross-section a title.

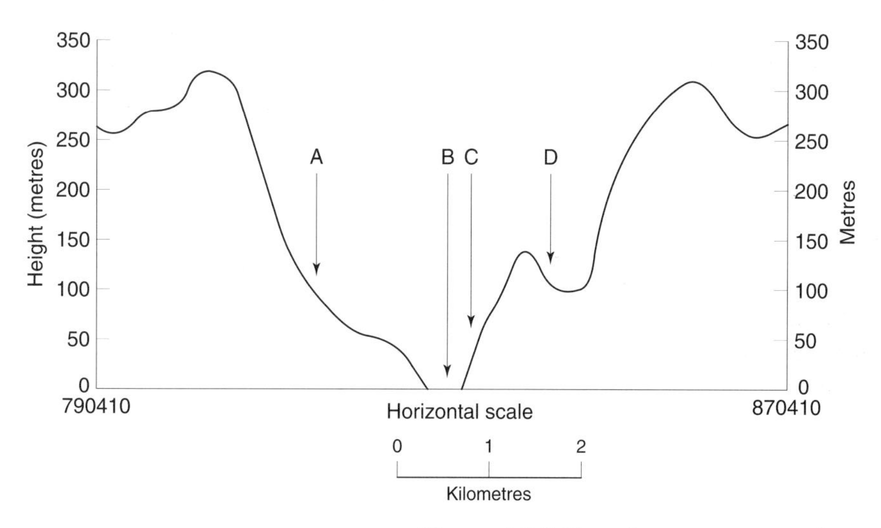

Figure 15.5 Drawing a cross-section.

15J DRAWING A TRANSECT

A **transect** is a line along which the location of features of the human or physical landscape are noted. On a map, a transect is used to show the land uses along a line and, especially, to show the relationship between relief and land uses.

- On the map, select a suitable transect line, which will clearly show differences in land use and relief.
- draw a cross-section, as described in 15H.

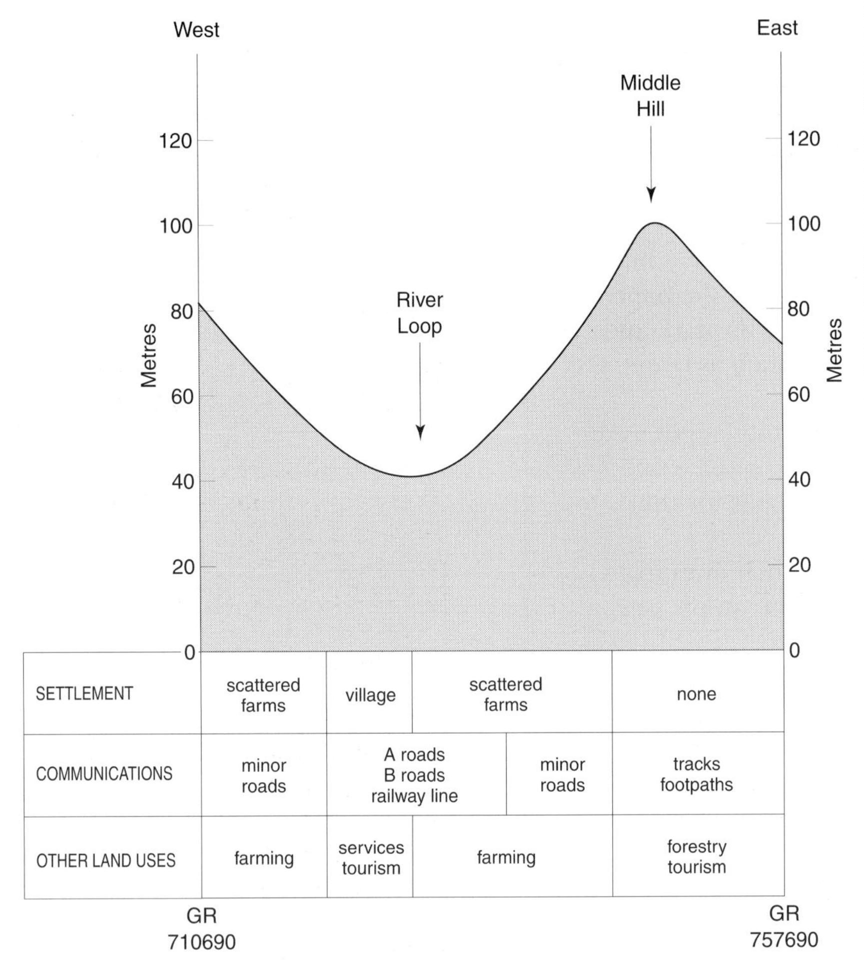

Figure 15.6 A transect across the Loop Valley.

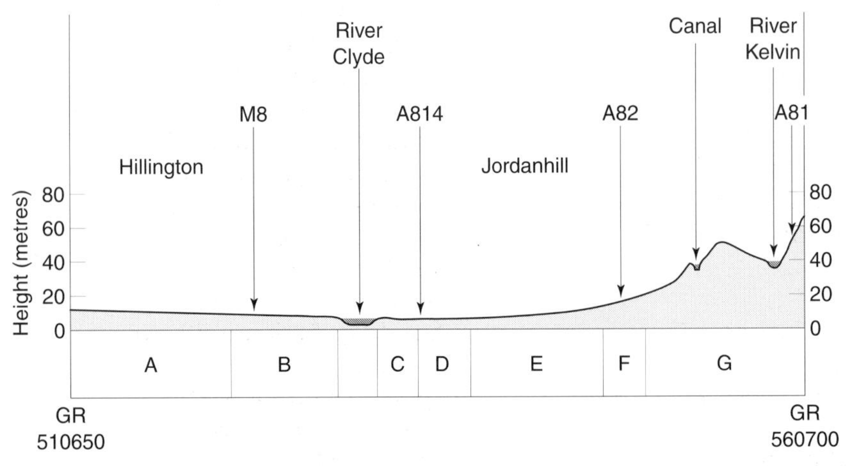

Figure 15.7 A transect across Glasgow from GR 510650 to GR 560700.

- underneath the section, draw several rows, one for each of the main land uses (see Figure 15.6).
- along each row, record the location of the different land uses as shown in Figure 15.6.

C Questions

Look at the OS map of Glasgow on the inside front cover of this book.

C1 (a) How suitable was the land at grid reference 581717 as a defensive site in Roman times?

(b) Describe the advantages and disadvantages of this site for early settlers.

C2 Using map evidence, describe the different functions of Glasgow.

C3 Where, in Glasgow, has the highest land value? Give a six-figure grid reference and justify your answer.

C4 Are the land uses in square 5862 typical of an inner city area? Give reasons for your answer.

C5 Name the following land-use zones A–G in the transect shown in Figure 15.7. Choose from: old low-cost housing, old industry, old middle-cost housing, new middle-cost housing, new industry, suburban business district.

C6 What is the most likely type of farming at Blackhill Farm (GR 573708)? Give detailed reasons for your answer.

C7 There is a science park at GR 556706. What are the advantages and disadvantages of this location for a science park?

C8 When the M77 was built in squares 5462 and 5361, it caused much conflict. Describe the different points of view that might have been put forward.

INDEX